# THE DIARY OF A NOSE

ALSO BY JEAN-CLAUDE ELLENA

*Perfume: The Alchemy of Scent*

JEAN-CLAUDE ELLENA

# THE
# DIARY
# OF A NOSE

## A YEAR IN THE LIFE OF A PARFUMEUR

*Translated by Adriana Hunter*

Rizzoli
ex libris

First published in the United States of America in 2013
by Rizzoli Ex Libris, an imprint of
Rizzoli International Publications, Inc.
300 Park Avenue South
New York, N.Y. 10010
www.rizzoliusa.com

First published in France as *Journal d'un parfumeur* by Sabine Wespieser, 2011
First published in Great Britain by Particular Books,
an imprint of Penguin Books Ltd., 2012

2013 2012 2011 2010 / 10 9 8 7 6 5 4 3 2 1

Distributed in the U.S. trade by Random House, New York

Printed in the United States of America

ISBN-13: 978-0-8478-4042-7

Library of Congress Catalog Control Number: 2012942495

*To my wife, Susannah*

*Smell is a word,*
*perfume is literature.*

# CONTENTS

*Pleasure*

I don't feel comfortable talking about pleasure; I find it easier to talk about desire. Since I started composing perfumes I've learned, I've invented 'catchphrase-smells,' like the first sentence, the first notes of a piece of music, the initial images that are reworked at length to capture a reader's, a listener's, a spectator's attention. So that he or she wants to carry on, in order to pursue the pleasure. In a society where speed is everything, perfumes are judged in a couple of seconds, as if at a glance. The hastiness of these assessments upsets me: a perfume can only truly tell its story when it is smelled and worn.

I like pleasures when they are shared, that is my definition of luxury. I transpose this ideal on to the perfumes I create, which are mostly meant to be shared by men and women. If I compose a 'men's' fragrance for a wide audience, I never fail to slip in some women's ciphers, and vice versa for a so-called 'women's' perfume. Fashion's codes were invented to be transgressed, to be played on; so I don't believe perfumes should be for women, for men, mixed or unisex. It is the people who wear them who give them their gender. In India, men have been wearing Yves Saint Laurent's *Opium*, Guerlain's *Shalimar* and Dior's *J'adore* since they were launched. I avoid pigeonholing, putting things in boxes, I would rather give people the freedom to choose, to appropriate each of my creations for themselves.

Pleasures, small pleasures: I like the pleasures we pilfer from everyday life, they brighten the day. They are mundane, they feel repetitive, they reassure. If we overlook them we deprive our-selves of the joys that make life bearable.

I take pleasure in composing, but some mornings the pleasure just isn't there in that little bottle. Physically, chemically, the draft of the perfume is the same – same temperature, same combi-nation of raw materials, of molecules – but smelling it affords me no pleasure at all. This fills me with feelings of despair and loneliness, and I have to suppress them. Sharing these misgivings with anyone else would mean condemning the work I've been doing for weeks, so when this happens, I put the bottle down and forget about it for a few days. I know that the initial pleasure, the idea I was pursuing, will come back to me.

On the plane, Saturday 31 October 2009

*Giono*

I'm on the shuttle, heading for Nice. My laboratory is in Cabris. My only luggage, one bag and one book: Giono's *Les trois arbres de Palzem*, a collection of the chronicles that were not included in the Pléiade edition of his *Récits et essais*. When I feel 'lost,' I read Giono to set me back on track. He works his way inside me, acts as a point of reference. Funny, the French for 'of reference' – 'de repère' – sounds like 'd'heureux père,' 'of happy father;' yes, he acts as a happy father to me. When I read his work, I mouth each word silently to myself. I need to hear the music of his words in my head, the rhythm of his sentences, the silences.

I like his writing, his inventiveness, his sensuality; and, when he talks about smells, I admire him. His passages about literature resonate with the way that I 'write' perfumes. I think that smells are signs, and that a perfume enthusiast interprets these signs as the perfume develops on his skin or on the fine sliver of a test blotter. He smells it, pursues it, abandons it, comes back to it; I can't say whether it is the perfume or the enthusiast who is beholden to the other.

As a perfumer, when I want to evoke a smell, I use signs that – taken separately – have no connection with the thing I'm expressing: there has never been any tea in Bulgari's *Eau parfumée au thé vert*, mango in *Un Jardin sur le Nil* by Hermès, or flint in *Terre d'Hermès*, yet the public 'feels' they are there. To cite Jean Giono, 'all the work of expression takes place in the reader's mind; from that he derives his pleasure and the satisfaction, gratification and joy it gives him.'[1] Although perfumers are traditionally compared to musical composers, I have always felt like a writer of smells.

---

[1] Our translation. All further translations of quotes are our own.

Cabris, Monday 2 November 2009

*The workshop*

I was back in the workshop this morning. An architect's house, it was built in the late 1960s in the spirit of concrete architecture, which strives to link buildings with their natural environment. Here, the outside is inside, and the inside extends outside, each conditioning the other. The house clings to grey rocks and is surrounded by a wild garden planted with Salzmann's pines. It could feel austere, yet is anything but. The sun filtering through the pine trees floods the workshop with soothing light. Time passes more slowly here, the seasons more noticeably. I love this place. I feel in tune with it.

A visitor looking at my desk would find it littered with dozens of tightly sealed little bottles, test-blotter-holders shaped like windmills, a worn file filled with a hundred formulae, a pot of coloring pencils, boxes of junk, a photo frame. Still, it can't be called a mess so long as I know where to find the formula for the draft I stopped working on a few months back, the grey crayon that I need, the box with the worn pencil eraser and the paper clips, not to mention my glasses – the ones for reading and the ones for distances. For me this 'mess' is connected to memory. When everything is organized, I forget.

Behind the desk – a varnished beechwood table from Ikea – is a chair that I use the way the travel agent does his in Jacques Tati's *Playtime*: everything is within reach by shuffling a few steps. From there, I can look out to the Mediterranean. Actually, when

I'm lost in smells and formulae, I don't see anything, but I know the sea is there. I just have to stop smelling, stop writing and look up for a moment to appreciate it.

Cabris, Friday 6 November 2009

*Pears*

I emerge exhausted after creating a perfume. The decision is made at last. An international launch is planned for next April. There were a substantial number of trials and drafts – several hundred – which is an indication of how difficult it is to find a guiding line, a form that expresses the concept. The project is bold and demanding; the bottle a technical feat. Then comes the fear that it won't find an audience. Each new olfactory story is a gamble.

Obviously, I have other projects on the go, but the work feels bland, it lacks breadth, presence and identity. I'm glum. I decide to take the afternoon off. I call my wife and suggest spending a bit of time in Italy (which is only an hour's drive away), sharing a plate of pasta and stocking up on groceries at the market in Ventimiglia. The market there is an institution. It operates every Friday and sells produce that is not only in season but in that very day, such as snails and mushrooms (provided it rained the previous Tuesday or Wednesday), not to mention Italian delicacies that can't be found anywhere else. We particularly like the great variety of dried mushrooms, the sundried, sun-blush and preserved tomatoes, and, most of all, a Parmesan cheese more than seven years old. This week several stalls are selling winter pears, small crimson-colored pears whose fragrance reigns over the market. I bury my nose into a fruit display, taking the salesman by surprise, and he says: *'Signore, guardate ma non toccate'* (Sir, you can look but don't touch). I tell him I'm just smelling. The smell is huge and obvious, and I'm suddenly startlingly aware that it could be useful to me. I experience such happiness, stealing the smell like this, that I note down how I feel, the names of raw materials, impressions, the beginnings of a formula. My memory will fill in the details I haven't written. The olfactory portrait I draw up in the laboratory later won't be a reproduction of what I smell here, but the image of that smell committed to memory. These 'olfactory encounters' that I turn to my advantage give me such a boost that I forget how tired I am and instantly feel light and free.

Cabris, Saturday 7 November 2009

Le Monde

I have a subscription to *Le Monde*, like at least two other people in the village of Spéracèdes where my family have their home and which has a population of almost a thousand voters. I know about these other subscribers because the postman has already wrongly delivered the newspaper twice, which gave me the opportunity for a brief chat with him about his round.

The painter Soulages made the headlines in *Le Monde* on Friday 16 October when a major retrospective of his work opened at the Pompidou Centre. In his interview, Soulages mentioned painters in the 1950s who tried to express their emotions and give their canvases meaning, a concept he doesn't understand. 'You can't possibly give them a definitive meaning: meaning comes together then comes undone,' he explains. He also explores the question of time, the inexplicable fact that a work several centuries old can bowl viewers over even though it surely no longer expresses the painter's intentions in his own era or in the place where it was created.

I remember having a similar experience, not to do with time but with meaning. In the early 1980s I ended up in China, commissioned to assess the production facilities of a Chinese perfumery factory for the company who employed me, who wanted to set up a partnership. A 'joint venture' was the precise term – which amused me, because I actually felt I was setting off on an *adventure* in a country I found intriguing, fascinating, and which

I knew only from tourist guides. Twenty-six years later I'm still fascinated by China. At the time, Shanghai was like a colonial city. Millions of black bicycles travelled along wide avenues lined with plane trees, amid a deafening clamor of shrill bells mingled with the piercing chirp of cicadas. Only officials travelled by car, their vehicles invariably black with smoked glass windows.

The apartment we had been allocated by the Ministry of Industry had plain 1930s furniture; the floor was covered by a thick silk carpet with a colorful pattern. Calligraphies in simple frames hung on the walls. I was especially taken with one of them, so much so that my eyes clouded with emotion. Although I couldn't hope to understand its meaning, given that I couldn't read the symbols, I was drawn to its blackness, to the upstrokes and downstrokes, to the sequence of shapes, but also to their rhythmic patterns. The experience is still vivid. Over time, I allowed myself to believe that my emotion derived from an intuitive feel for how the hand had worked, the choreography of gestures, which was an extension of the body and of thought.

I don't think I've ever truly managed to break away from meaning. Perhaps I don't want to if 'abstraction' implies a wish to be completely free of representative signs. Yet I like abstract painting and certainly don't idolize reality – far preferring the imaginary, illusion, delusion (in the playful sense of 'inventive' rather than 'deceptive'). For years I've kept a diary of olfactory notes, the result of silent solitary experiments, a quick guide to smells, lists of two to five components that I juxtapose to create olfactory illusions to be used as and when I need them. Using this technique, I have reduced smells from everyday life and the world around us to the smallest olfactory expression. Nature is complex – there are five hundred molecules in the smell of a rose, more for the taste of chocolate, fewer for garlic. I have engaged in this game to free myself from natural representation, using it to establish what amounts to olfactory semantics so that I can combine these signifiers in complex smells, in perfumes. I am conscious of the fact that the work on which I build my 'olfactory suggestions' doesn't bear the reassuring seal of recognition or approval.

A few examples of my 'delusions':

>     LILAC
>     phenyl ethyl alcohol
>     helional
>     indole
>     clove buds (essence of)

Phenyl ethyl alcohol and helional alone can produce the smell of early-season white lilac. For the flowers in full bloom you need indole, and purple lilac needs traces of clove.

Or, more simply, starting with the essence of sweet oranges:

>     BITTER ORANGE
>     sweet orange oil
>     indole

## BLOOD ORANGE
sweet orange oil
ethyl maltol

Cabris, Monday 9 November 2009

*A preface*

Among my current commissions is the preface to a book devoted to hands, vines and wine. I like this sort of work, which
forces me to focus on a subject I don't know and, sometimes,
to establish links with my profession. I accepted the commission in memory of a trip through the Bordeaux region during
which I renewed acquaintance with a talented photographer. I
am receptive, as a craftsman and artist, to anything to do with
hands and, as a man, to the trust people put in me, the homage
they pay me: in short, I don't want to disappoint. But for three
weeks now I've been sitting at my computer going round in
circles. I'm looking for a way in, an angle, a point of view that
resonates with the purpose of the book. I swivel in my desk
chair and catch sight of a book I particularly like on the man-
telpiece: François Jullien's *Conférence sur l'efficacité*. I open it at
random at page 55. Jullien is discussing action and transformation. The Western world favors action while the East prefers
transformation. I read a few lines. I've got my angle: the art
of transformation. Hands at work are hands involved in every
form of transformation.

Paris, Tuesday 10 November 2009

*Movement*

I've been invited by a debating society called the Friends of the Paris School of Management to the 48<sup>th</sup> session of their seminar on 'Creation' to share my experiences as an artist and craftsman. The time is set for 8.45 a.m. on the dot at one of the top engineering schools in France, the Mines de Paris. I'm impressed by the venue and intimidated by the twenty-five people there. The only qualification I have is a school certificate I was awarded at thirteen, and I'll be speaking to men and women who went to the prestigious and highly competitive grandes écoles. My 'conference' revisits the major themes of a layman's guide to perfume I've written. There is a screening of a short film about my experience of creating *Un Jardin après la Mousson* for Hermès. After the presentation people ask me a lot of questions.

I like questions about my profession; they mean I have to understand my own thought processes in order to reply, and they take me to another level. One particular comment really struck me and still probes me long after the conversation:

'You've told us about how you structure your thoughts, about the form a perfume takes, about time and composing perfume, but you haven't said anything about movement.'

I was not able to tackle the subject of movement; I had very little time left and I have to admit that I didn't have a clear answer to the question. This diary is an opportunity to make up for that. Movement is defined by the form a perfume takes and its longevity. So a more baroque perfume is all about complexity, power and performance. Its complexity follows its evolution, enhancing each new phase. Perfumes like this are seen as elaborate, structured, rich, full and perhaps overbearing. Conversely, a cologne-type structure favors simplicity, vigor and lightness of touch – although not all colognes are simple; the rapid succession of notes within them makes us think they don't stay on the skin for long. This sort of easily accessible perfume requires a very particular attention because its discretion keeps such lovely surprises in store.

Cabris, Wednesday 25 November 2009

*A visit*

As a person, I take pleasure in receiving and sharing. As a perfumer, I like showing and convincing; the only problem is that I make myself play a role. I'm both the same and not entirely the same individual. The need to please, to seduce, sometimes makes me alter work in progress and tend more towards fulfilling a demand – a decision which is satisfying at the time but will start niggling at me the very next day.

Although in everyday life I'm drawn to exchanges of ideas and enjoy confrontation, in my work I need solitude.

I don't create using comparisons. Often, I don't evaluate the new draft by comparing it to the previous one. I only want to see whether the overall olfactory result corresponds to the idea I have in mind. The painter Turner explained that he painted dozens of watercolors of the same subject at the same time, all from memory, and in the end kept only one, destroying the others. My approach is similar. For me it's not a case of changing a few elements in a perfume's formula in a linear progression towards a known goal, as a practiced craftsman might when perfecting a piece, but of striving for something that doesn't yet exist. So, after a while, I stop and smell all the drafts, keeping only two or three (each of them with its own form of expression and not the result of the one before), and discarding the other trials. That is how I open up new territory. In fact, I'm quite simply following the trajectory of an artist, someone who seeks and, sometimes, finds.

Messina, Tuesday 1 December 2009

*Quality*

I have a meeting with the R family, who own the company Simone Gatto, which specializes in producing essences of citrus fruits; their essences of Sicilian lemon and mandarin orange are bewitching, as is their essence of Calabrian bergamot.

Sandro R and I are talking about quality. He's telling me about meeting Lanvin's perfumer André Fayasse in the 1950s, to make a presentation for an essence of bergamot obtained using a new process. The perfumer smelled the sample and announced that he had to turn it down, saying that the smell of this new essence didn't correspond at all with the one he usually used. Intrigued by this rejection, the young Sandro made some inquiries and discovered that the essence of bergamot produced for Lanvin was obtained by packing parings of zest into a knotted muslin which was hung up by a rope so that the force of gravity made the essence drip down into a varnished terracotta vase below. The parings fermented overnight, giving a 'distinctive' note that the perfumer saw as a sign of quality, while the new process avoided such fermentation or oxidation. We laughed together over this story, which illustrates perfectly how difficult it is to change our reference points and our habits.

Obviously the quality of materials used in perfumery is essential. Quality is a commitment; it should be sought after, for it is an integral part of perfume, but it cannot in any circumstances be considered to drive creativity. The most beautiful raw materials do not the most beautiful perfumes make.

Essence of bergamot made in October is of different quality to essences produced in the months of November, December, January and February. Production is carried out for five months of the year and actually results in essences that start off with intense, fresh, green notes and continue with floral and gustatory notes. October essence has the highest content of linalool, a constituent with a floral smell, and February essence has very little linalool but contains fresh-smelling linalyl acetate. Thanks to tiny quantities of cis-5 hexenol, however, October essence is perceived as fresh. In February essence, molecules of cis-5 hexenol and linalool diminish in favor of linalyl acetate. Nature plays with our sense of smell, because it is only when it is used in compositions that the floral aspect of October essence versus the fresh aspect of February essence can be identified.

Messina, Wednesday 2 December 2009

*Standardization*

Up until the 1980s I used products that few perfumers would dare use in their perfumes now, such as last residue forms of methyl ionone, hydroxycitronellal or lilial, all manufacturing by-products whose smells are difficult to reproduce identically. I used reproductions of natural musk, composed of disparate ingredients whose quality could not be assured with certainty, making the production of perfumes unreliable. Since then, products have been standardized, and there is less hapless tinkering taking place. Oddly, this standardization, which should be a rationalizing process, led to a degree of 'waste': even though they are not toxic, these by-products have now been eliminated because they cannot be standardized for production on an industrial scale.

Messina, Friday 4 December 2009

*The unrefined smell*
We left early this morning to catch the ferry across the Strait of
Messina to Villa San Giovanni in Calabria. We have a meeting
with a farmer who produces unrefined essence of bergamot
in the village of Condofuri. M. P. meets us in the courtyard of
his home-cum-factory. To the left, the family home – which
houses his children, their wives and his grandchildren – rises
up over three stories. To the right, the factory, a building of
the same height. Vilfredo R. has asked me, out of courtesy for
his employees, to take photographs of outside the factory only.
He is a short man with a square head, a tanned face dotted
with liver spots, thick grey hair and direct, piercing black eyes.
He is wearing worn, dark trousers of indeterminate color, and
a navy blue quilted jacket of indeterminate age.

M. P. greets us in his own language. I only understand one
word in three. He proffers his hand, the firm hand of someone
familiar with the land, then leaves us to go and talk to our guide.
Long rambling discussions ensue several feet away. After quarter
of an hour of negotiations, we are invited to see his machines
and to smell the essence he produces. The smell manages to
smother the impressive racket of the machines; it bowls me over,
floods through me. In my work, I usually try to establish some
distance from smells, the better to grasp them, to understand
them, to smell 'behind' them, but here it penetrates me, I can't
get away from it, I let it wrap itself around me, let myself be

clothed by it. It feels like the olfactory equivalent of a mono-chrome image. The pleasure of this unrefined smell is well and truly a physical experience, an experience in which thought is eclipsed.

In the afternoon we visit the *giardini di bergamotti*, the berga-mot orchard – in southern Italy orchards where citrus plants are grown are called *giardini* (gardens) – which gives me an oppor-tunity for a whole new experience: smelling the fragrance given off by bergamot plants in December, a smell of fruit zest rather than flowers, as with orange trees. In the course of conversa-tion, I learn the names of the different varieties of bergamot: *Femminello*, *Fantastico* and *Castagnaro*. A scant knowledge of the language suggests these names refer, respectively, to women, the spectacular and chestnuts; you need only look at the fruit to understand the names. I also learn that misshapen fruit is called *meraviglia*, marvel. This name delights me, particularly as these mistakes of nature are given pride of place on tables and side-boards because they are thought to have magical properties.

Cabris, Monday 7 December 2009

*A pear, or the outline of a perfume*
I have returned to the workshop and my beloved phials. While
I was away, I left experimental formulae on the theme of pears
to be weighed up later. The young green top notes are very
appealing. To the pear theme, I've added floral notes but without the heavy, narcotic characteristics typical of white flowers,
and a chypre accord, a composition of patchouli with woody
and labdanum notes, which should play like background music
as the perfume develops. As I write these few words to describe
the perfume, I realize I'm the only person who can conjure its
smell mentally. In this diary I could easily reveal various elements that composers of perfumes would be able to decipher.
Even so, giving away the composition of the outline I have in
mind would not make readers any the wiser about where I'm
going with it. My ideas are evolving constantly. I don't know
in advance what might be corrected by experiences from the
past, nor what those of the future have in store for me.

To the uninitiated, discovering a perfume from a list of its raw
materials is like reading the ingredients for a cooking recipe
with all the frustration of not being able to imagine what the
dish would taste like; images seem to create more of an echo
in us and speak more fully to our senses. Marketing people understand this perfectly. Seeing advertisements has never meant

being able to smell the perfume; at the very best it elicits a *desire* to smell it: such are the strengths and limitations of the exercise.

Paris, Friday 18 December 2009

*The Pygmalion myth*
I have been invited by one of the foremost producers of fine perfumes to gain an insight into market trends. Although I never try to analyze the market, drawing information from the street and the Métro as to which perfumes are worn, I am curious to see this study. The presentation about trends is based around a classification of perfumes. Images of the bottles are projected on to a screen while test blotters impregnated with each perfume are passed beneath our noses. I'm shocked, saddened and disgusted. Too many perfumes are alike, merely variations of models that sell well.

The choice of perfumes depends on marketing directors; they make a selection that is then tested on consumers alongside one or two perfumes already on the market. These act as benchmarks, and facilitate a comparative analysis of preferences.

This sort of procedure dates back to the 1970s when the commercialization of perfumes ceased to be governed by a company chairman's choice and was entrusted to a marketing team, who first assessed 'market needs.' Today product managers or project managers not only advise perfumers about what to make, they also want to choose the people who will execute their concepts. By choosing young perfumers with whom they can identify, they turn themselves into Pygmalions. Convinced they have 'good noses' while paradoxically relying on market trials, they exhaust the abilities of these young creators by asking for more and more daily samples and not respecting the time needed for evaluation and reflection.

I like to think that every perfumer considers his or her work an art, and that a desire to create constitutes the motive for this work, because the perfumer is the first to appreciate the emotional investment he or she has put into the project. Unless freely chosen, collaborations with other perfumers can only do the utmost harm to a project. Even if the exchange itself is beneficial, the accumulation of ideas is an utter negation of any creative process. Dividing up the personal investment in order to lighten the emotional load that goes into a project means misunderstanding the techniques used and developed by a perfumer in response to a commission. This sort of attitude and process cannot fail to engender frustrations which will later become difficult to manage.

Cabris, Tuesday 5 January 2010

*Mint*

The launch of the 2009 annual theme for the House of Hermès, 'L'Échappée belle',[2] took place in April at the Rungis market, the largest fresh-produce market in the world. In the early hours of the morning, as guests emerged from the covered market, they were asked to fill a basket with fruits and vegetables of their choice. I remember putting bunches of fresh mint in my basket. The smell acted effectively as a joyful and soothing energizer. I still remember in great detail this 'olfactory encounter,' which I recorded in my moleskin notebook, and have now decided to start work on it.

The theme may be self-evident, but its interpretation is adventurous. There are many essences of mint in perfumery – spearmint, peppermint, pennyroyal, field mint, bergamot mint – which are also used for flavoring sweets, toothpaste, chewing gum and sometimes as fragrance in household products; these different applications depreciate the emotional impact of smelling mint. The same is true of the smell of lemons, which was first used as a fragrance for dishwashing liquid in the United States in 1969 on a product called Joy, and went on to become an olfactory symbol for cleaning products. Since then, lemon has only rarely been used in eaux de toilette. In order to transform

[2] This play on words sounds like the expression for 'a narrow escape,' and also implies a wonderful moment of escape.

mint into a perfume, I therefore need to find a new setting for this smell, which for me conjures up streams and fountains.

Eaux de toilette on the theme of mint do exist or have existed, for example Jacques Fath's classic *Green Water* and, more recently, Heeley's *Menthe Fraîche* in the United States, but none of them corresponds with the idea I have in mind. My trials begin with an accord of iris and spearmint: it is a remarkable and pleasing contrast, but that is its only quality. On the fifth trial I abandon this line of research. I set off again with an accord of tea and spearmint: the harmony works, but it is too reminiscent of herbal teas. Eight, nine, ten, eleven trials; the mint-tea theme will not be followed up.

Paris, Thursday 14 January 2010

*Classic*

Late in the afternoon, I drop into the FNAC store to buy a few Maigret paperbacks for a handful of euros each – a pleasant evening lies ahead. I take the opportunity to buy a bilingual (Italian–French) version of Collodi's *Adventures of Pinocchio*, a choice guided by my wish to start learning Italian again. I usually leaf through the books I buy, homing in on sentences at random. Collodi's book is a classic, as Italo Calvino defined the term: 'A classic is a book that has never finished saying what it has to say.' This definition is one I adopted as my own a long time ago. It reminds me of a particular incident which must date back – although I cannot place it exactly because I don't have a chronological recall of the events in my life – to the time when I was starting to earn a little money as a young perfumer. I had treated myself to a watercolor by a young American painter called Betsy N., whose husband was a family friend. The watercolor was a floral composition in a Japanese-inspired style that I found delicate and cheerful. Pleased with my purchase, I had it framed and hung it somewhere that I passed frequently so that it could intoxicate me as often as possible. After a fortnight, the watercolor emptied itself of all content. It no longer spoke to me. Brought back down to earth and nursing my wounded pride, I stopped looking at it. In the end I took it down and forgot about it. How could I have been so utterly seduced and so rapidly tired? How could I ensure my perfumes weren't reduced to a single reading like that? At the time, I was starting to use 'working drawings' to map out the complexities of my formulae, and I turned repeatedly to Edmond Roudnitska's *L'Esthétique en question* for inspiration and guidance.

Paris, Sunday 17 January 2010

*Dizzying lists*

Under the direction of Umberto Eco, the Louvre Museum put on a modest exhibition on the theme of lists – an exhibition which, in relation to the whole museum, was about the size of a cupboard. It was called *Mille e tre* (a thousand and three), in reference to Don Giovanni's servant Leporello singing of his master's exploits in Mozart's opera.

Computers are tremendous prescribers of lists, so much so that they provide lists of lists; having all that knowledge of the world at your fingertips is dizzying. Oddly, though, lists are reassuring. We become aware of this if we scrupulously follow a recipe, which is essentially a list of ingredients and actions; but if we give this 'list' too much importance, we leave no room for the imagination. For a perfumer, lists are part of everyday life: lists of usable materials, prices, banned substances, recommendations. The formula for a perfume also appears in the form of a list of raw materials to be weighed out in a specific order; however, unlike with a recipe, once this particular list has been established it tolerates no changes for fear of modifying the perfume. One of the lists that I find disturbing is the list classifying perfumes: the perfumes referred to have a date of birth, but no date of death; they sometimes appear followed by the word 'obsolete' – never 'out of stock,' which I would prefer.

Written out like this, the list of perfumes – some of which were created a century ago – does have some meaning: it shows that, out of a hundred or so creations from one perfumer, only three or four perfumes go down in history. It can also be read as a lesson in humility.

*Slowness*

Two women are queuing to watch Jane Campion's film *Bright Star*; one turns round and, seeing me in this mainly female crowd, she says: 'This isn't a film for men.'

'Do you think there are different films for men and women?' I reply.

'It's a slow film, men prefer action, results; they can't take slowness.'

'You should spend some time with different men.'

'Tell me, do you think that beautiful stories should be told slowly and silently?'

'I . . .'

The crowd starts moving again. This little exchange brings a smile to my face.

Paris, Monday 18 January 2010

*Shazam*

Shazam is a music recognition app for an iPhone that almost instantly supplies the user with the name of a song or piece of music. It's an astonishing app but it does have its limitations – although they do nothing to detract from its technical prowess. This evening, while listening to some Brahms on the radio and not managing to name the piece being played, I seize on this app. My request fails. Shazam cannot help with my inquiry because the recording was made in front of an audience and doesn't feature on any disc. No official track, no recognition. Shazam cannot accommodate approximation. Decoding by approximation is something we all do, all the time. When I walk through Paris, I obviously don't know every street but I manage to locate where I am by using visual approximation, thanks to a shop, a monument, a distinctive building; or sometimes olfactory approximation, the smell of a *boulangerie* or a grocer's shop. It is the same with odors that I come across in the street. At a distance, the trail of a smell feels familiar; I identify a form, and the closer I get, the more details I glean. In the end I place it, and sometimes name it. I do sometimes get it wrong if the perfume is 'in the style of' or a copy.

*

*'A wink of the nose'*

I am reading *The Nose*, a short story by Nikolai Gogol. In this
unusual comic tale, Major Kovalyov 'finds' his nose again on
the 7<sup>th</sup> of April, a date which fortuitously happens to be the
one on which I was born.

Paris, Saturday 23 January 2010

*Show*

I only rarely take up the invitations I am sent to go to fashion shows. But I do particularly like the ones put on by my friend Véronique Nichanian. She likes the men she dresses. Her work is a combination of rigor and casualness. I can feel the pleasure she derives from different materials and the subtle interplay of colors. She likes grey, every kind of grey; I can't think of a more delicate color or one more difficult to work with. Sometimes she plays on contrasts and ventures into audacious combinations with cardigans, shirts and jumpers in cadmium yellow, Prussian blue or poppy red.

Among the audience are a number of journalists who came to the launch of *Voyage d'Hermès*. They have some very flattering things to say about the perfume and find the exact words to describe what I wanted to express. Even though this is all I could wish for, it leaves me amazed. I may be susceptible to compliments, but I know that in the end it's the general public who choose. For the hundred or so new perfumes launched every year, you have to wait six months after the first sales – the restocking period – to know whether a perfume has some chance of success. *Terre d'Hermès* is the fourth bestselling men's fragrance in France, a great achievement for a company that does not have the promotional facilities of large cosmetics groups. I can't explain this success, just as I can't explain the lack of success of *Un Jardin après la Mousson*, which I believe is one of the most beautiful floral compositions I have written. The financial rewards of a success are not an explanation, but a statement. As for any desire to find a simple explanation for success or failure, it derives from a wish to be blinded.

Paris, Tuesday 2 February 2010

*Mœbius*

For the launch of *Voyage d'Hermès*, we asked Jean Giraud, aka
Mœbius, to do some drawings on the theme of travel for the
new perfume's press pack. It was a wonderful idea. Our modes
of expression are different, but both encourage a meeting of
minds. We get together at the offices on the Faubourg Saint-
Honoré. He's a man who talks freely, full of humor, and we
soon feel like partners thanks to a preoccupation we have in
common: 'a clear line.' He tells me how, when he started out
in cartoons, he loaded his pictures with detail, but as he grows
older he is more and more inclined to use a clear line, which
implies a perfectly distilled drawing, luminous, sharply distin-
guished colors and a spare linear narrative.

I explain that I have a similar approach, and ask him to smell
the perfume. He smells it and can sense this intention. 'It smells
very good!' he says. 'It's a relief being able to tell you that. I was
worried I'd have to pay you compliments out of courtesy, and
that would have bothered me.'

Cabris, Wednesday 3 February 2010

*Naming*

I receive a telephone call from the project manager concerning the naming of a new creation, a divertimento based around iris flowers, which will be available in shops in the autumn. The theme may seem banal, for it is often used by perfumers. I avoided this trap by working on the scent of the flowers whose fragrance is actually not well known, hovering between notes of roses, orange blossom and mandarin; a cool delicate perfume that is fragile and yet assertive.

Being a collector of Japanese engravings, I'm picturing images of irises in the floating world, such as the famous *Irises* folding screen by Ogata Korin. As an echo of this world, my garden blooms throughout May and June with white and blue irises, from snow white to feather white, from blue black to azure blue, with a few touches of pink. The two worlds interpenetrate each other and I cannot see, smell or touch an iris without my responses being affected by the interpretations of Japanese artists.

The names of all the Hermessence perfumes comprise the name of the raw material that is at the perfume's origin and one other word that defines the spirit of the composition. The research is done by associating ideas, or occasionally raw materials. In this instance, juxtapositions with Japanese words seem appealing: iris *Kon'iro*, the second word denoting the color blue; iris *Kado* or 'the path of flowers'; iris *Ukiyo-e* or 'image of the floating world.' The names iris *Hiroshige* or iris *Hokusai* cannot be used; they have already been registered. A name is a sound that should resonate with all your senses; it is the first point of contact with the perfume. This is why it takes several months to choose one, particularly as the search for copyright registrations is international, and sometimes goes on forever.

Cabris, Saturday 6 February 2010

The Princess and the Pea

Pages two and three of the latest *Nouvel Observateur* carry the new advertising campaign from the House of Hermès on the theme of fairy tales. *The Princess and the Pea*, an Andersen tale, is the first picture in the series. In a full-page image, a young woman with braided hair and wearing a brightly colored silk scarf rests her head on a pile of cushions with multicolored designs whose perky invigorating shades remind me of sweet peas.

In the background, the sky, a landscape, a hazy world of smooth uninterrupted lines. The pile of cushions and its juxtaposition of green, yellow, pink, mauve and blue are allegories on the theme of harmony. They emanate a cheerful seductiveness that I would like to recreate in the women's perfume I have in draft form, the one that takes an evocation of pears as its starting point.

Cabris, Monday 8 February 2010

*Mint again*

My usual suppliers have offered me different forms of mint obtained using a variety of distillation and extraction processes. Essences, because they are distilled using water vapor at more than one hundred degrees Celsius, lose the green notes of crushed leaves. Absolutes, which are made using dried vegetation (the inclusion of water being unsuitable for this type of extraction), smell like straw or cut hay, which is not right for this project. Extractions using carbon dioxide, because they are produced at extremely low temperatures, come closer to the smell of freshly chopped mint. Among those on offer, I am drawn to one product but, because it contains a lot of chlorophyll – a pigment that is spinach green in color – it will need work to remove the color. For, although I would like a 'green smell,' I want a colorless perfume, in order to have an element of surprise.

For the Hermessence perfume *Brin de Réglisse*, I decided to combine the liquorice ('réglisse') of the name with lavender. I used essence of lavender and intervened to modify its composition, which includes several hundred different molecules, so that I could have an ingredient in keeping with the idea I so coveted. In this instance, the composition of mint essences is not very complex, and I have no wish to modify it: the major constituents and those responsible for the smell are principally carvone or menthol. Carvone is the flavor of minty chewing-gum, and menthol that of minty sweets.

Alongside this research into ingredients, I am experimenting with new accords using the samples at my disposal. I am playing on the contrast between the cool greenness of mint and the dark suffocating qualities of patchouli: a surprising combination.

*Anguish*

I am no stranger to ill-defined, unexplained feelings of anguish. I never invited them in. They appeared out of nowhere when I was twenty years old or a little less. I loathed them, then accepted them. Much later, it was this anguish that led me to understand that 'the true mystery of the world is the visible, not the invisible'. This quote from Oscar Wilde, which is both simple and complex, shook me so profoundly when I first read it that I felt I had completely lost my footing for a few seconds. It was as if I were on the edge of a gaping abyss, empty of all knowledge; then this fleeting sensation dazzled me, it seemed like proof of an undeniable alertness, affirming my existence.

Anguish always surges up without warning, but I recognize the early signs. When I am composing perfumes, it most often appears when I start a project. So it is not unusual for me to feel choked with anguish when I read the first lines of a formula I have just written. This formula, reduced to just a few lines, produces a panicky feeling that I will run out of ideas, run dry. In fact, I feel an animal need to tackle each creation with a 'pared down' response (if that does not sound too presumptuous), as if stripped of facile automatic responses, of the reflexes that clutter up creators' lives, particularly more experienced creators. Sometimes those first lines are the product of pure impulse, a short-lived urge, but more often than not they are dictated by an attempt to transcribe a more extensive and elaborate project. In these instances, they represent a frightening promise that I have to flesh out with my intentions and desires.

A quite different anguish grips me when I am creating one of the Garden perfumes. The fragrance I am composing does not start with an abstract idea that I have to bring to life, but with the place I am in and the premise I choose. Choosing – from a whole palette of possibilities – a smell or smells to act as signals means setting off down a path that I will have to mark out for myself; the anguish is relative to the choice. It entails sleepless nights. Some might say that the choice is personal and does not work for everyone, and I readily accept that. And yet I believe that international exchanges are globalizing tastes and therefore our sense of smell, so that we share common predilections despite a few personal aversions.

Once I have chosen the path the anguish disappears, and then I am entirely wrapped up in the pleasure of bringing the perfume into being, of writing it. Sometimes it does return, though, when the time comes to make the final choice.

Moscow, Monday 15 February 2010

*'The grass is always greener on the other side of the fence'*
I am in Moscow for the launch of *Voyage d'Hermès*. I am sitting
in a hotel lounge and ask the waitress for some black tea. She
offers me a selection from Hédiard. In the same standard of
hotel in Paris, I would have been served Kusmi Tea, a Russian
brand. Fernand Braudel was right when he wrote that capital-
ism was 'a game of exchanges.'

Moscow, Tuesday 16 February 2010

*A gift*

I am interviewed by a journalist who asks me whether I have a gift. I understand that to mean a talent, an innate ability, a natural advantage. I reply that I couldn't define talent, let alone what is innate or natural, so no, I don't have a gift.

I chose perfume by chance, or rather perfume chose me. I could have been a plumber, a painter or a musician, but no one around me was a painter, a plumber or a musician. That is not completely true: my uncle, my mother's brother, was a music teacher in a state school. I remember that when I was a teenager, and we were living in Nice, I went to him once a week for a few months to have a go at playing the piano, using Ernest Van de Velde's *Rose Essor Piano Method*. I can still see the colors and art-deco graphics on its cover. But no one at home took any interest in my progress. It was a different story when, at sixteen, I went to Antoine Chiris's company in Grasse, a factory that was the official supplier to the famous house of Coty for the first half of the twentieth century.

I went into perfumery as if into a religion, joining a firm that occupied the premises of a former Capuchin monastery. My habit was blue overalls. It was only later that I wore a white coat. Then that in turn was put away in the early 1970s: May '68 had come and gone. There I met men and women who took an interest in me from the start, and who steered my first steps; with this support, I made progress. I was interested in everything, distillation, extraction, research, manufacturing, analysis, buying. But I was not at all drawn to accounting; finance felt out of reach and far too serious. It was the beginning of an apprenticeship, a tentative process of exploration – one I still use today: that is how I became who I am. At the age of nineteen I left Chiris to fulfill my duties in military service. I had no idea what I would be. I just hoped that, when I came back, there would be a place for me in this world that I loved.

Since then, the Chiris facilities have been destroyed and their old premises now house the local law courts.

Cabris, Friday 19 February 2010

*'Nebulous'*

I am home from Paris. I am listening to France Inter on the radio and a word suddenly catches my attention: 'nebulous,' spoken by a young writer who has been asked whether he is planning another novel. He replies, 'I have just one page, there's an idea there; it's nebulous, but it's all I need.'

Later in the evening, I open the book I am currently reading at page 141. As I turn the page I come across the word 'nebulous.' The word is following me. Nebulous is the idea I have in mind for the women's perfume I have started work on. I know only that I want something floral, fruity and appetizing. Appetizing but not edible. Edible smells are lazy; something appetizing is exciting. 'Appetizing' is a word sufficiently evocative to be turned into a smell.

Cabris, Sunday 21 February 2010

*Gardens*

I am thinking back to a question I was asked, at the 'Creation' seminar at the Paris School of Management, about whether I needed to visit the actual location when I was creating the Garden perfumes.

When Hermès gave me the option, I remember saying it was not absolutely essential, a description of Leïla Menchari's garden would be enough to fire my imagination. I thought my talent alone could identify the olfactory premise for the perfume that would become *Un Jardin en Méditerranée*.

In the end, the company insisted I went there in person. I accepted. Before leaving I read nothing about the place so that I could tackle the project with an open mind. All the same, I expect I took a Giono paperback with me on this adventure as a talisman, to help ward off my usual feelings of anguish. I was given a kindly welcome. The garden I discovered was nothing like the one I had imagined sitting at my desk. Just as people take a box of watercolors with them to make sketches, I arrived with a wealth of smells in mind – North African flowers, fruits and woods – but no knowledge at all of the concept, layout or personality of an Arab garden.

Beneath the cedars, eucalyptuses and palm trees shading long alleys, all my senses were bombarded. I was lost. My imagination was suddenly under assault and was soon taken prisoner by commonplace responses, banalities that I had to forget so that I could learn to see the play of light and shade, smell the fig tree and the sea daffodils, listen to the song of water features and birds, touch sand and water. It took me three days to find and choose the premise for the perfume, to find the best way of expressing the shadiness and cool of that unique place.

Cabris, Monday 22 February 2010

*Mint, still*

Discoloring mint by extraction using carbon dioxide gives a clear, pale yellow liquid just as I wanted, but accentuates the cut hay/dry grass aspect that I don't want in this composition. I decide to work using only traditional essences of mint, favoring spearmint and pennyroyal, whose unrefined smell I find enchanting. I put to one side the spearmint-patchouli harmony for a future eau de toilette: it is a dark harmony better suited to that form of interpretation, whereas a cologne should be more vivacious and afford instant pleasure.

I could work on a harmony of mint-petitgrain-bergamot-lemon, with the aim of achieving a classic cologne, but that construction lacks inventiveness and feels too banal to me. I try a new harmony by altering the proportion and intensity of each component. The blackcurrant base and the spearmint, which I use in abundance, have some common notes of equal intensity that harmonize well. Triplal is a powerful molecule with a hard, raw, green smell that needs handling with care. This compound gives an impression of cut leaves. By overdosing it in this composition, it partners and masks the spearmint's 'chewing gum' effect.

The blackcurrant-spearmint harmony was first used in *Eau d'orange verte* for Hermès, but at the time it was just one of the characteristics in this chypre composition, and not its dominant character. Here, the idea is to bypass the citrus elements so that there is simply a startling impression of freshly cut mint: the first drafts are interesting.

Cabris, Thursday 25 February 2010

*Fashion*

I do not consult the stars but readily turn to the nebulous blogosphere. There are a good many blogs that consider perfume to be an emanation of fashion, and yet the principles governing these two universes are not fundamentally alike. Perfumes and fashion may go hand in glove and may appear together in public but they do not live together. The timetable for couturiers' collections does not follow the same rhythm as the development of a perfume. Perfume, in fact, avoids the short-lived fate of fashion. Fashion is, by definition, something that will be out of fashion. Because hundreds of perfumes are launched every year, it would be easy to see this as a fashion phenomenon, for only a rare few stand the test of time. Once bought, most perfumes are used up and forgotten. Only perfumes that emancipate themselves from this constraint become 'fashionable.' With perfumes, time creates the fashion and engenders inclinations, and it does this despite the efforts of the Escada brand, which has opened up the way for short-lived perfumes by offering an olfactory novelty every year.

This free association between perfume and fashion serves to stabilize a brand's name, its signature. Perfume acts as a counterpoint to the transient enslavement exerted by fashion.

Cabris, Friday 26 February 2010

*Trend*

The ogre economy needs feeding. It has a fierce appetite and refuses to tighten its belt. And yet it has no curiosity, is not attracted by novelty, and always wants to be served the same dish: trend. Its relationship with trend is both obvious and a paradox. In order to accept it, the ogre economy needs to be told the same stories – stories about ogres – over and over again, and to have trend pumped up with talk and magic rites and tests. Trend, on the other hand, likes to have competitions laid on, beauty competitions, all sorts of competitions, because it wants to be accepted. It has to be referred to humorously, even ironically – it's not afraid of self-mockery. It surrounds itself with groupies and bloggers and chatter.

Tocqueville anticipated the fact that, in a democracy, society would tend towards unified tastes. Trend may be the price we have to pay for democracy.

Hong Kong, Wednesday 3 March 2010

*A bowl*

A bowl with a slightly trapezoid base and no embellishments; the concept of a pair of hands cupped to hold water. A serene shape, stripped of any opinion, without an author. A bowl with a pure design, drawn with one stroke of the pen. It is white in color, white as snow in sunlight, as a cloud in a clear sky, limpid and luminous. It stands out from the other bowls in the glass display case. Its outline and color are accomplished, and give me a feeling of elation. An object, as the painter Chardin wrote, 'has an inner truth – I would say a resonance too – that we reach only through feelings.' The description says simply: 'Bowl, eggshell porcelain, Ming dynasty, XVth century, Museum of Art, Hong Kong.' 'Bowl' – the practical implications of the object remind me of Kant, to whom beauty could exist only outside usefulness. According to him, an object cannot be described as beautiful. Every piece of pottery exhibited in this museum is a refutation of that very Western judgment. From terracotta to ceramics, in China as in Japan, pottery has always had an influential role in art and craftsmanship; so much so that some pieces have been elevated to the ranks of 'national treasures.' This bowl in itself is a definition of beauty.

Hong Kong, Friday 5 March 2010

*Artificial*

'What's that artificial thing?' someone asks. The thing or, rather, things are white cubes, slightly larger than sugar lumps, dotted with black flecks the size of poppy seeds, and mixed in with diced apple and watermelon, and slivers of mango and orange – this is a fruit salad offered as part of the hotel breakfast. The 'thing': cubes of dragon fruit, a fruit with pink skin and white flesh that is very popular in Asia but, to us Westerners, has little taste. It is ignorance that makes us believe and announce that something like that is artificial, when the familiar clearly seems natural.

How many times have I heard someone say: 'Your perfumes only have flowers and natural products in them, don't they, nothing artificial?' A question to which I invariably reply that I use just as many artificial products as natural ones, and that without artificial products I would not be able to create perfumes.

It was the chemistry of perfume that allowed the artisans of perfumery, towards the end of the nineteenth century, to become artists by freeing themselves from the constraints of nature.

Hong Kong, Saturday 6 March 2010

*Disappointment*
I brought in my hand luggage the draft for the women's perfume with pear as its top note. Being somewhere else is a good way to smell something differently. I vaporize the perfume and smell it. I am disappointed. Is it because of the heat and humidity of Hong Kong, or is my nose playing tricks on me? The smell is rasping, acrid, a distortion of the idea I had in mind. I close the bottle and put it away in my bag. I will smell it again later.

Tokyo, after the plum trees have blossomed
but before the cherry trees have

*Juxtaposition*

Seasonality has a cultural dimension in Japan. It is customary
there to begin a letter with a reference to the season, to dress
in the season's colors and to eat according to the cycle of seasons. This evening we have been invited to dine in a restaurant
that cooks soba, noodles made with buckwheat flour. We have
the restaurant to ourselves. The place is the size of a small
lobby. The smell of flour is very noticeable and reminds me of
roasted chestnuts. We sit down at a counter made of cypress
wood. We are greeted by three cooks in their whites wearing
blue bandanas round their foreheads. They are at our service,
here to prepare dishes and serve them to us. One of them
kneads the dough and leaves it to stand for a while. He then
picks it up again and, following a precise ritual, spreads it into
a square shape. Then, using a ruler, he cuts away noodles the
thickness of a shoelace. Meanwhile, another cook mills grain
of buckwheat with a pestle and mortar, making the flour that
will be used for the next sitting. The noodles are thrown by
the handful into the hot stock kept at the ready and removed
almost immediately, shared out between our bowls and served.
The meal begins. I am advised to take big slurps. Noodles are
eaten noisily in Japan.

After the first bowl of noodles, there is a succession of many
other dishes, each presented in different tableware – in Japan

tableware changes according to the season: ceramics in winter, glass and bamboo in summer. And each new offering is a surprise to the eye and the palate. Each concoction plays on the juxtaposition of colors, textures and tastes, and on the seasonality of the produce. The freshness of the ingredients is essential, the flavors are subtle. In this sort of cuisine, over-piling the plate, extravagance and sauces are unknown. Mixtures, which are typical of traditional Western cooking, allow for correcting mistakes. Here mistakes are not allowed. The performance played out before us contributes to our pleasure, a temporal hedonistic pleasure, and requires excellence from the cooks.

Kyoto, Wednesday 10 March 2010

*Courtesy*

We are leaving the *ryokan* this morning; the owners of the
inn see us out on to the street and thank us at length, leaning
their torsos forward, straight-backed. We set off in the taxi and
travel a few meters. I glance back and the owners wave to us
once more, keeping a watchful eye on our departure. I hesitate
to look away. We lose sight of them when the taxi turns at the
end of the street.

We need to take the Tokaido Shinkansen, the high-speed line
that will take us to Kyoto. I am impressed by the size of the station, by its cleanliness and signage, thanks to which a foreigner
has no trouble finding his way. When we reach our platform,
I am surprised by how calm and disciplined the other travel-
lers are: each passenger waits silently between the lines on the
ground indicating where the carriages will be. The train arrives.
We settle into the seats that we reserved in France. A vague waft
of *Chanel No. 5* hangs in the carriage, and I turn round to find
out who is wearing it. There are only men in the carriage. Could
the air conditioning be perfumed? The ticket inspector checks
our tickets. He turns to us, greets us with a tilt of the head, then
leaves. He comes back at every stop and greets us every time.
The woman selling drinks pushes her trolley between the seats,
dressed like a schoolgirl, white blouse and black skirt. She has
put on a purple and yellow apron tied at the back with a pretty
bow. When she reaches the automatic door, she turns round and

she too leans her torso forward, with her back straight, her eyes focused on the tops of the seats.

Whether it is on arrival or departure, in hotels or inns, in cafés or shops, to the Japanese salutations are a day-to-day mark of courtesy. Courtesy is not a virtue – these small acts of courtesy, which can appear artificial and even false, almost make me want to smile – but it is a quality, a ritual that facilitates life in society, and one that I appreciate.

Kanazawa, Monday 15 March 2010

*Natural*

After spending a few days in Kyoto, the city with two thousand palaces and gardens, the place people cherish in their memory when they are in love with Japan, we take the train to Kanazawa, known for its garden, which symbolized ideal beauty in the days of the Song dynasty. Whether they are rock or moss gardens, or gardens simply to stroll in, Japanese gardens seem artificial to our Western eyes. Of course, to our Japanese guide there could be no more natural gardens. I remark on the layout of the garden, the choice of stones, the use of water, the refined way the trees are pruned, the contrived arrangement of branches right down to thinned-out pine needles, bough by bough, on the symbolic beauty, whose composition makes full use of the surrounding landscape – but when I comment on all this she maintains her pretty smile and good humor, and tells me that it is all natural. What is natural is therefore cultural.

Tokyo, Friday 19 March 2010

*Bill Evans*

Talking about jazz in Japan might seem incongruous. It is not at all. Jazz is part of Japanese culture. There is a Blue Note in Tokyo.

Apart from Starbucks outlets, which favor rock, most cafés and meeting places greet you with the sound of jazz, with a preference for the jazz of the seventies and eighties and often groups of three or four instrumentalists. Restaurants, on the other hand, prefer classical music, Debussy and Mozart. And, although Mozart may feel out of place to me in a country that eschews extravagance, Debussy or Ravel are perfectly in keeping with it. A people that listens to jazz is a people that favors human exchange.

A jazz lover myself, I walk into the famous Yamano Music shop in the Ginza district hoping to unearth a recording I have not heard of Bill Evans, whom I think is one of the greatest pianists of the genre. I find a rare DVD. Back at the hotel, I slip the disc into the Sony player and listen and watch as the trio play: Bill Evans, Marc Johnson and Joe La Barbera. There is in Bill Evans' playing a sensitivity, a precision, a presence and a clarity that make me love humanity. His 'sound colors' are reminiscent of Gabriel Fauré's and Claude Debussy's.

I would like to transpose those 'sound colors' into 'olfactory colors.'

Cabris, Monday 22 March 2010

*Works in progress*

I am back in my workshop this morning, and at my table, where a number of projects are in progress. There are three colognes based on different themes waiting for me there. One, the mint cologne that I have already mentioned, I have put aside for now. The second is a cologne based on elemi – the citrus-smelling resin from an exotic tree. The third is based on mandarins and I have christened it *Eau de mandarine bleue*, a playful title inspired by the poet Paul Éluard, although he preferred oranges.

I also have a new Garden perfume underway and have christened it *Un Jardin sur le Toit*, a homage to the terrace at 24 Faubourg Saint-Honoré, which, during the Second World War, was a vegetable plot intended to provide some produce for the Dumas-Hermès family, and was transformed into a garden when Jean-Louis Dumas took over as chairman of the company. A garden made up of white flowers through the seasons, roses, irises, pansies, impatiens, tulips, not forgetting the pear tree and apple tree.

The women's perfume whose draft disappointed me in Hong Kong – but with which I still have an affectionate relationship – may yet turn into something.

I am also working on the Hermès classics *Calèche* and *Bel Ami*, which I am interpreting like jazz standards, with my own sensibilities. I have named them *Vétiver de Calèche* and *Cuir de Bel Ami*.

I could mention other work, such as *Bois amer*, B*ois de pierre*, *Fleur de porcelaine* and *Narcisse bleu*, that may never see the light of day.

For now all these perfumes are 'in progress.' Although their names do not reveal much about the form I have in mind for each of them, but they make it easier, once I have set them aside, to find them again. Of course, I could have assigned them codes or numbers, but I prefer names, names are one of the keys to their stories.

Cabris, Thursday 25 March 2010,
after listening to the writer Patrick Modiano
in *L'Humeur vagabonde*[3] on France Inter

## *Temperament*

Up until the 1970s, perfumes prided themselves on being accomplished works. They were complex rather than structured;
they were piled high, an accumulation, an addition, and af-
forded only one reading. There was a sort of pretention in
this, a desire to dominate that tolerated no criticism. I followed
this model when I composed *First* for Van Cleef & Arpels in
1976. Gorged on analyses of market archetypes, I collected,
borrowed and conflated every signal for femininity, wealth and
power into this perfume, which, over time, has become alien to
me. I certainly do not disown it. The loving relationship I had
with it lasted only the time it took to create it.

With successive creations, the way in which I conceive perfumes has changed. I no longer listen to the market – creativity
sometimes needs a deaf ear. I no longer pile in components, I
juxtapose them; I no longer combine them, I associate them.
My perfumes are accomplished perfumes but not finished ones.
Each perfume is linked to the one before and already features
the next. That is not to say that they are alike, but they are united

---

[3] This translates approximately as 'the wandering temperament.'
Originally the title of a 1971 film by Édouard Luntz , it is now the
title of an arts show on the France Inter radio station.

by subtle connections. I never take an existing formula as my starting point. Every formula is forgotten once the creation is completed. In fact, I work from memory on variations on a few themes that are special to me; I try to revisit them, correct them and take their form of expression further, somewhere else, in a different direction. None of which means I do not look for new themes. Charles Trenet said that of the thousand songs he wrote only a dozen were successes to his own ears.

This approach does not imply a desire on my part to impose on people, but a constant need to awaken pleasure and curiosity, and create an exchange. So I deliberately leave gaps, 'spaces,' in perfumes for each individual to fill with their own imagination; these are 'appropriation spaces.'

Paris, Tuesday 30 March 2010

*'Shrewd'*

I am at the Paris book fair with Gérard Margeon, who is Alain
Ducasse's sommelier, and the philosopher Chantal Jaquet, to
talk about smells, wine and perfume. Gérard Margeon expresses his hope to see wine tasting go beyond a purely figurative conversation. Citing notes of raspberry, blackcurrant, oak,
rose or leather is only a starting point. This sort of vocabulary
is used in the first stages of apprenticeship, but it needs ex-
panding with references to location, soil, mineral content and,
most importantly, the man who makes the wine. A wine's character should express the temperament of the man who makes
it, otherwise the wine is condemned to responding to market
demand and simply pandering to the palate, in other words to
repeating itself, using the same formulae to seduce the maxi-
mum number of people, and becoming a 'lowest common de-
nominator' that no longer really expresses anything. I can sense
his longing to set wine free from the canons of taste, which establish its typicity once and for all. This discussion delights me
and reinforces my views. I intervene to tell him that – unlike
a wine master, who proceeds by assembling the various types
of grape, sorting, measuring and adding them – I proceed by
subtracting, in order to simplify my perfumes. Where the master of wine is concerned, man adds to nature; as a perfumer, I
remove myself from nature to reduce it to the level of signs.

Chantal Jaquet invites the audience to understand the world

through their noses, and not just their eyes, and to question their prejudices about our sense of smell, such as how weak it is and how underdeveloped. She quotes at length from Nietzsche, who said that to philosophize was to 'have a nose.' The word 'shrewd' recurs frequently in her talk about our sense of smell, and it stirs my curiosity. That same evening, I have fun looking up the definition for it and finding synonyms for it on my computer. A 'shrewd mind' is a mind with the ability to grasp things quickly, through intuition and acuity of thought. But there is an element of sixth sense to it too, of sniffing things out: perspicacity, discernment, intuition, insight, sensitivity, subtlety. All of a perfumer's art summarized in a single word. So could you say perfumers are characterized by this ability to sniff things out, this 'sixth sense'? The idea is both amusing and gratifying.

Cabris, Wednesday 7 April 2010

*Canons*

Listening to Gérard Margeon setting himself the task of
freeing wine from the canons of taste – canons that are con-
tinually exported and imitated, returning to us as an echo of
themselves, standardized by other continents – made me think
about perfumes and the history of perfumery.

Until the 1970s perfumes had to comply with standards dictated by bourgeois aesthetics and budgets inherited from the
nineteenth century, following the rapid development of the
chemicals industry. These standards were defined by the composition of a perfume, the olfactory family it belonged to and
its concentration. The composition was determined by the inclusion and choice of accords of different notes: floral, woody,
green, spiced, etc. The chief olfactory families were floral, orien-
tal, chypre, citrus and fern. Perfume concentration was defined
in terms of how the perfume was used. What is more, apprentice perfumers had to be familiar with some forty archetypes
that represented the aesthetic canons of perfumery. By defining
these rules, standards and aesthetic canons, perfumers were in
possession of a repository of knowledge akin to an inheritance,
a tradition and a national identity.

The only real innovations of the 1980s were the use of new
products, be they chemical or natural, and a technique seen as
revolutionary: the 'headspace,' which made it possible to analyze
the smell of flowers in situ, although the resulting information

hardly made a convincing contribution in terms of creativity. Perfumery companies were becoming international and shifting from perfumery that had something to offer, to one that responded to demand; this globalized tastes. The rare few innovations likely to give the French market leaders something to think about came from the United States. They included the introduction of the smell of cleanliness, as well as the smell of prudishness, thanks to the widespread use of vaporizers, which were in some senses a natural consequence of prudery (a gesture made far away from the body, gadgetry substituted for the erotic). They also included a tendency to judge a perfume's marketable value principally by its intensity and staying power.

It is difficult to classify a perfume nowadays. The raw materials used in perfumes, most of them chemical in origin, are moving away from references to 'nature.' The aesthetic approach to composition is no longer a question of adding different accords but a vision of a whole, which means perfumers can fully master its expression. Regrettably, a perfume's performance – its diffusion and intensity – too often takes precedence over elegance, with the sole aim of making it more accessible and of gratifying an international clientele.

Commercially speaking, old perfumes are no longer venerated, only newcomers are considered. The ten bestsellers in France are recent perfumes, with the exception of *Chanel No. 5*, Guerlain's *Shalimar* and Yves Saint Laurent's *Opium*. Within the industry, the future does not really lie in discovering new fragrant raw materials. On the pretext of increasingly strict legislation, of development costs and the countless compulsory safety checks, the budgets allocated to research have been reduced. Chemical manufacturers, who favor molecules with familiar smells that can be produced by the ton, contribute less and less to widening perfumers' olfactory palette.

In order to endure, *haute* perfumery is therefore condemned to inventing new olfactory premises, a new style of writing, to redefining quality, to finding a new form of expression and a new way of behaving towards those who still believe in it and need it. It is only if it is able to meet these exacting requirements that the craft of composing perfumes will reclaim its full meaning and value.

Paris, Thursday 8 April 2010

*Sweet peas*
I am walking along the rue Royale. I stop by the window of the
florist Lachaume. I have just spotted sweat peas in every color.
I like their fragrance. I take out my mobile and call Anne, my
assistant, to ask her to order some from Coquelicot, the florist
in a village near Cabris.

Paris, Friday 9 April 2010

*Leïla*

Leïla Menchari is exhibiting window displays at the Institute
of the Arab World – recognition for a profession that is both
beautiful and futile, and one we need because it allows us to
dream, which is very important. I first came across her displays
on the rue du Faubourg Saint-Honoré in 1993, at a time when
I was head perfumer for a German company. My office was
opposite the house of Hermès and, four times a year, mem-
bers of staff would go out into the street at the end of the
afternoon to watch the curtain being raised on the main window display. Later, when I was taken on by Hermès, I met
up with Leïla, whom I had first encountered in her garden at
Hammamet, near Tunis. She encouraged me to look at and feel
leather and silk goods, objects whose value owes everything
to a deep knowledge of the raw material and to the precise,
measured, repeated gestures of the craftsmen who work with
them. Leïla knows the colors that bring them to life and the
gestures that make them enchanting.

Paris, Saturday 10 April 2010

*Beauty*

I am making the most of this afternoon in Paris to see a Lucian Freud exhibition at the Pompidou Centre. I discovered his painting in 1995 at an exhibition at the Maeght Foundation that was dedicated to him and Francis Bacon. A large proportion of his work is devoted to nudes. The choice of life-size canvases makes them all the more immediate and alive. His models bear no relation to the aesthetic canons of ancient or classical beauty. They are like me; they are ordinary and, even though they may be disturbing at first glance, they eclipse themselves in favor of the painting itself; it is not the models that I see, but our bestiality and our humanity. Even if his work has a place in the tradition of figurative and realist painting, Lucian Freud is never one for seduction, illusion or appearances, either in his subject matter or with the colors he uses, and that fascinates me. Particularly as this sort of representation is diametrically opposed to my creative approach, which is enjoyable and seductive. And what if the enduring appeal that Lucian Freud's work has for me were simply a feeling of love with no desire for possession?

Cabris, Wednesday 14, April 2010

The Princess and the Pea, *continued*

This morning, waiting for me on the table that I use as a desk,
are bunches of white sweet peas. I would have preferred them
in bright acid colors: orange, pink, green, mauve and blue,
but in terms of fragrance the white ones are preferable. The
colors in the advertising campaign – *The Princess and the Pea* –
reminded me, by association of ideas, of the colors of sweet
peas, and, conversely, when I walked past Lachaume's window
display, the sweet peas reminded me of the advertising image:
the smell of these flowers could become a possible theme,
even if only a partial one, for a women's perfume.

When sweet peas are gathered in a bunch, they remind me
of the ruffles on flamenco dresses. A single flower on its own
is slender and its petals have an organdie quality. They do not
have a definite smell, but one that hovers between roses, orange
blossom and Sweet Williams, with their hint of vanilla. I scribble
down the seven components I think I will need to sketch the
smell. One, two, three trials to balance the proportions, and I add
a note of carnation to the fourth trial, and then go on to correct
that too. The fifth trial feels right to me. I now have the outline
of a fragrance with which to start a perfume.

SWEET PEA (trial 5)
phenyl ethyl alcohol                          200
Paradisone®                                   180

| | |
|---|---|
| hydroxycitronellal | 50 |
| rhodinol | 30 |
| acetyl isoeugenol | 15 |
| orange blossom (colorless absolute) | 15 |
| cis-3 hexenol | 5 |
| phenyl acetic aldehyde 50% | 5 |
| | ——— |
| | 500 |

To be smelled as a 5% solution in 85° Celsius alcohol.

Cabris, Thursday 15 April 2010

*Green*

My suppliers of raw materials visit me at regular intervals to show me products of chemical and natural origin. I enjoy dreaming a little with them. They know me, and know that I like to smell them diluted to weak concentrations, and that there is no need to come with demonstration formulae. On that particular subject, I remember one supplier who came to make a presentation and, intending to flatter me, had reproduced one of my creations and had substituted one of its components for a different component of his company's own design. Although sincere and naïve in its intention, this irritated rather than touched me. Imagine a paint salesman coming to see you with a reproduction of one of your paintings, and trying to prove to you that his green is better than yours. I could under- stand if it were the color of a door, a wall or the front of a house, but not in a painting.

Today I am seeing the perfumer and the commercial representative from a particular company; they show me traditional products obtained using new extraction techniques, as well as an extract of nasturtium leaves and flowers. I find its green smell arresting and intriguing. I have been looking for new green notes for years. Of course, this absolute conjures up the green notes of nasturtium leaves, but also wasabi, horseradish, capers and bluebells. Its green smell is candid and unlike any other, it has something to say for itself. I do not choose a raw material only on the grounds of the quality of the smell, but also for the possible uses I anticipate for it.

Green is the only color that makes sense as a smell. In my collection of raw materials, which is not arranged in a discriminating way with better ones and worse ones, I have different kinds of green: gentle, harsh, smooth, sharp, dense, etc. I have greens that smell of beans, fig leaves, syringa, ivy, seaweed, elder, boxwood, hyacinths, lawns and peas. Although I may not know of yellow, red or blue smells, I do know the characteristic smells of white and yellow flowers and those of red fruits.

Moustiers-Sainte-Marie, Wednesday 21 April 2010

*The classics*

We are all here to define our vision and the strategy we want to put in place for the years ahead. One of the issues we discuss is our old perfumes. Hermès is one of the rare perfumers to have continued selling its entire range of perfumes since they were created. The first, *Eau d'Hermès*, was composed by Edmond Roudnitska in 1951. I feel a particular affection for this perfume. It represents the early beginnings of a man who was to put his stamp as a perfumer on the third quarter of the twentieth century. Its formula is complex, unstructured, but contains a jumble of all the accords and ideas to follow. Five years later he composed *Diorissimo* for Dior, an archetype of refinement and a paragon of the smell of lily of the valley. Lily of the valley may be Christian Dior's favorite flower, but I can only explain Edmond Roudnitska's dramatic change in the way he composed perfume by the fact that he now worked for himself. He had left the De Laire firm, which specialized in making synthesized products, to set up on his own with his wife, and to found the company Art et Parfum.

The 'classics' – a lovely way of describing our oldest perfumes – represent only a small percentage of our sales, with the exception of *Calèche* (the Hermès logo is in fact a *calèche* – a horse and carriage). The economy and the retail strategy favor the young, and they have no use for the older perfumes. I am shocked by this because they are all beautiful perfumes. All the same, I do not feel that the industry has a duty of memory which would mean that, a century from now, *Terre d'Hermès* should necessarily still be for sale – the International Museum of Perfumery in Grasse has that task – but it has a duty of respect. I like the thought that a man or a woman can choose a perfume at twenty and is still able to buy it when he or she is sixty, having indulged in a few infidelities.

Moustiers-Sainte-Marie, Thursday 22 April 2010

*Craft*

In the space of five years every single person involved in de-
veloping the perfume collections has been replaced. These
people, with whom I shared a vision, and who were in charge
of our work strategy, have all left their jobs. I find this disconcerting. Within a company employees don't stay long in a
particular job. It is true that a position can, by its nature, foster
a need for change because, after a while and despite the variety
of the work, tasks become repetitive, producing a feeling of
boredom and a loss of interest.

Apart from the economic problems relating to salaries,
changes produced by the constant remixing of personalities are
probably a simple way of taking a fresh look at things. Without
wishing to negate this, I do think that such a quasi-quantitative
vision should be replaced by a more qualitative approach based
on improving the value of the job; based, in other words, on
apprenticeship and skill development.

As a perfumer, I do not have an actual job, but I practice a
craft, one that involves knowledge, know-how and skill. And
yet that in itself is not enough: in order to continue to exist and
to practice my craft, I have to keep re-inventing it and not just
repeat any old recipes.

Unlike a 'proper' job, which is quantifiable, a craft is always
extending its field of operations, pushing the boundaries of the
craftsman's abilities ever further. Inventing means renewing,
growing.

Cabris, Tuesday 27 April 2010

Iris Ukiyoé

The name of the new Hermessence has been chosen. Having
hesitated for a long time between *Iris Ukiyo* and *Iris Ukiyoé*, I
chose the latter. The word *'ukiyo'* means 'the floating world', an
aspect of Buddhist philosophy that invites us to meditate on the
poignant beauty of fragile things. It teaches us that the world
is constantly changing, ephemeral, evanescent, and resists any
attempt to model it. This word *'ukiyo'* provides an echo of my
vision of the perfume; the additional 'é' implies a pictorial expression of this world and refers more specifically to Japanese
engravings. Here, the expression is olfactory. These engravings
attract our attention and awaken our curiosity because they de-
pict subjects drawn from daily life as the seasons go by: flowers,
landscapes and journeys – such as Hiroshige's *Fifty-three Stations
of the Tokaido* (the route connecting Kyoto, the imperial capital,
to Tokyo, the shogun capital). The same subjects, points of view,
blocks of solid color and successive layers to suggest perspective, and the same rhythm in the composition itself, were used
by painters in the late nineteenth century. I am very interested in
painted screens, particularly those representing *The Tale of Genji*.
A number of them narrate the lives of noblemen. They have
a geometric composition, gilded enclosures and clouds separat-
ing and organizing men and women's daily leisure pursuits. The
absence of roofs enables viewers to see right inside their homes
and to have access to the intimate details of a culture with an
acute sense of propriety, much influenced by the arts.

*Corso di italiano per stranieri*

Over the last few months, I have started studying Italian again, not with a view to using it professionally, but for the pleasure. The pleasure of putting myself in a position of ignorance and learning; learning a language, or any other thing, means opening yourself up to the world once more; it is also a return to humility.

I really like my young Italian teacher. He teaches in a private school in Nice, and speaks several languages including French, English and Spanish. Every Tuesday afternoon, he takes the bus to Grasse from the bus station in Nice, changes at Cabris and walks two kilometers to my workshop. It takes him nearly three hours – the same distance usually takes less than an hour by car. It is not so much the distance that matters as the journey itself. He does not complain about the wasted time. He takes pleasure in looking at the scenery, at sitting back and being driven. He reads and sometimes marks his pupils' work. This trick of calmly and contentedly apprehending time strikes me as altogether delightful and enviable.

The two hours we spend together are intensive and require an effort of concentration on my part. 'Luckily,' the teacher says, 'you have a musical ear.' I remember sounds, find it quite easy to understand what he says to me and to reproduce words correctly. The most difficult thing for me is listening to recorded conversations. Because it is impossible to interrupt them; I have to listen to these dialogues through to the end before trying to repeat the snatches I have understood.

In the early weeks, unable to practice because of my busy schedule, I was overwhelmed by a feeling of dissatisfaction and guilt. Until the day when I realized there was no need to feel guilty and that I should give in to the thrill of rediscovery. No school marks, no exams looming, just the pure pleasure of wandering through this language I so love, in the same way that I stroll along the path of various perfumes I am planning.

Late April, the month belongs to lily of the valley. It looks as if I am going to settle on the premise for a project, one I have been working on for several years, called *Fleur de porcelaine.*

Cabris, Thursday 29 April 2010

*Evaluation*

'You don't smell things the way we do!' How often have I
heard that during perfume evaluations! Taken at face value,
these words could mean that I am unique, that my nasal ap-
pendage is out of the ordinary; and I could find myself hauled
up to the summit, alone. But I could also view this pronounce-
ment as a humiliation, a rejection: 'You're different, you don't
belong in our world; how could you judge things the way we
do?'

No, I don't smell things the way you do. With the passing
years, for the sake of perfumes and for them alone, I have developed an analytical, methodical and distant nose, and, although
my curiosity may still be fierce and acute, I long ago stopped
feeling infatuated with a new discovery. I envy the emotion an
enthusiast experiences when he smells a perfume for the first
time, using words of love that I wish I could come up with again.

I do not expect technical comments from an evaluation,
nor for the perfume to be positioned in terms of the market;
I mostly hope for observations. I wait for people to appropriate the perfume, to experience it, judge it and get the feel of it
without thinking about the aims of the project, and to describe
it as a perfume lover would – one who responds to his actual
experience and describes his pleasure or displeasure.

Cabris, Friday 30 April 2010

Féminin H

My drafts for a perfume on the theme of pears have been waiting on the table for two months now. I smell the last trial and
rediscover the smell I so liked. I ask my assistant for a 'fresh'
solution of the concentrate that she keeps in a cupboard,
away from the light. When the sample is diluted it has a hard,
harsh smell. It will need to spend a long period of maturation
steeped in alcohol to achieve the rounded notes of pears.

What it says is appetizing, crisp, seductive but a little cold. So
I modify the pear accord to give it a juicier feel, and I highlight
the perfume's sensuality by intensifying the little trill of chypre.
I choose one of the trials and ask for a half-liter to be put aside
to mature.

The painter Cézanne said to Pissaro: 'With just an apple, I
want to amaze all of Paris.' There is a bit of that ambition in
what I am doing: I want to surprise and amaze with an everyday
smell.

Cabris, Saturday 1 May 2010

*Perfection*

I am with Jane, an American whose heart belongs in part to France, and we are talking about perfection.

'Can you achieve perfection in your work?'

'I think so, although I constantly question it.'

'How would you describe perfection?'

'I can't give you a definition. What I can say is that Christian culture sets up perfection as a goal to aim for, while at the same time introducing a notion of struggle and unattainability into this aspiration, because, to Christians, God alone can embody and represent true perfection.'

'I find that disturbing.'

'In the West, Christian culture clearly permeates views, and influences the way people see and judge things. In Chinese or Japanese culture, perfection exists, it is also a goal to aim for, but the aspiration isn't unattainable and isn't tainted by a sense of guilt. Buildings, paintings, sculptures and pieces of pottery are recognized as "national treasures" when they represent perfection. People, particularly artists and craftsmen with unusual skills, can also be described as "living national treasures." France may also describe works exhibited in its museums as "national treasures," but the term refers only to their value.'

Cabris, Friday 7 May 2010

*'Craftsman and Artist'*

Hermès is an establishment whose heart beats to the rhythm of its 'podiums.' Twice a year, in January and July, all the creative departments present their spring-summer and autumn-winter collections to a gathering of its own chairmen, directors, designers, craftsmen and artists, and to the world as a whole. July is nearly here, and I am being asked to write the text for next year's catalogue on the theme of 'Craftsman and Artist.'

Craftsman, artist: I have never managed to settle for one or other of these definitions for myself. I feel like a craftsman when I am completely wrapped up in making a perfume; I feel like an artist when I imagine the perfume I need to make. In fact, I constantly juggle with the two standpoints. If perfume is first and foremost a creation of the mind, it cannot actually be created without the mastery of true skill.

When I am creating fragrances for the Cologne collection, I am very much the craftsman: the raw material gives the perfume its meaning, even when I twist its characteristics by omitting citrus essences, which are traditionally indispensable to this form of expression. It was in this spirit that I constructed *Eau de gentiane blanche* around white musk – the name given to synthetic musk – by substituting the age-old olfactory signs for hygiene and cleanliness that are citrus fruits with those of today: white musks.

When I am creating the Hermessence perfumes – a collection sold exclusively in Hermès stores – I behave like an artist, with the raw material becoming a symbol for an idea. With these perfumes, although the names refer to the raw material used, the idea is to create something realistic (I like that word: the solid 'real' and the approximate 'istic'), that plays on realities and appearances, and acts as a good definition of my work.

Cabris, Tuesday 11 May 2010

*Journalists' questions*

Not a week goes by when I do not receive an interview by email. Apart from questions relating to the launch of a perfume, inevitably a brand new one, there are recurring themes: questions about the future, fashion, trends, upcoming launches, sources of inspiration, personal experiences, how to create a classic perfume (which I interpret: 'a perfume that stands the test of time'), how to choose and store perfume, the raw materials I use and, lastly, my likes and dislikes.

I have not always responded to interviews very willingly. As a young perfumer, they made me uncomfortable. My nose buried in a bottle, engrossed in my work, I didn't know how to reply. As I have matured, I have opened up to this sort of exchange, taking pleasure in the questions I am asked, seeing them as another opportunity to think about what I do, to take a step back and to hone my craft. Now I wait greedily for the one question that I cannot answer straight away, the one I will keep hold of or write down in order to think on it at greater length. Sharing information in this way deepens my love of perfume.

I like to think that when the 'beauty' press and blogs give information and share their knowledge about perfume, the general public becomes more susceptible to this form of expression. By understanding what they smell, by placing perfumes the better to discuss them, perfume enthusiasts share their pleasure and create the conditions for an addiction to perfume.

Cabris, Wednesday 12 May 2010

*An ordinary day*

Thank goodness, I also have ordinary days. On these days, I arrive in the office at about 8.30 in the morning. Anne has already rolled up the metal shutters on the large bay windows, and switched on the computers, the photocopier and the coffee-maker. Over a coffee, we discuss the tasks for the day, and any imminent visits, if visits there are to be.

Once at my desk, I start by evaluating the previous day's work on test blotters. I repeat this evaluation process with freshly dipped blotters. I make a note of the alterations, changes in proportions and increases or decreases in raw materials. To keep a sense of perspective, I work on three or four themes at once. I work out what I am going to do on paper. I prefer paper because it gives me an overall view of a formula and means I can make annotations in pencil. I leave it to my assistant to calculate costs and check that my work complies with current standards, which she does on her computer when the information is needed. When the final modifications have been made, I give her the formulae. While she gets the various elements together and sets the production process in motion, I screen my emails, read those that have escaped the deleted bin, and reply to written interviews. The only interruptions to my work will be a few telephone calls with Pantin, where the Hermès offices are located.

Once the trials have been made, I unscrew the bottles, sniff them and dip the ends of blotters into them. I smell trials with one long inhalation lasting several seconds, hunched over the bottle to be at one with the perfume. I breathe out and my body unfurls. I smell it again. I compare the trials, flitting from one blotter to the next. I 'inter-smell' the range of possibilities, feel encouraged, then select what I want to keep. Lastly, I write down the formulae and correct them. More work begins. I leave the selected trials on a blotter-holder at least overnight so that I can see how they evolve and can rectify possible flaws in their composition. Sometimes, when I fail to pin down my thoughts, I postpone the work for a few days. Depending on the project the number of trials varies from a handful to hundreds – quantity is not connected to quality or vice versa. We break for an hour for lunch. Then I leave the workshop and go for a long walk; this gives me a chance to air my nose, which is simply a testing tool, and to put my thoughts in order again. The after- noon is similar to the morning. Sometimes, caught up in the round of trials and new finds, I lose track of time and my assistant follows suit. However, more often than not, ideas fail to appear on demand.

Paris, Friday 14 May 2010

*Censorship*

A real boon, when you have lunch at Ladurée, is to be able to order one of their boxes of macarons without waiting at the register. You simply ask your waitress for a slip to fill out with the flavors you have chosen and how many you would like. Your order will be waiting for you when you leave. We make our choice: a box of twenty-four in various flavors, salted-butter caramel, coffee, praline, chocolate, raspberry, orange blossom, lily of the valley and mimosa. My wife is curious about the lily of the valley and mimosa flavors, and asks whether – given that tastes and smells are so inextricable – it is possible to invent tastes that do not relate to an existing perfume. In reply I tell her that the amber used in perfumery was not originally a reference to a smell with natural origins, despite its name; it was actually produced by combining vanillin and labdanum, and presumably derives its name from the color of this combination.

It is now difficult to open up the way for new tastes and smells, because we live not only in a world where traceability is of key importance, but at a time when everything has to be justified. Inventing a smell as innovative as amber in perfumery, or the taste of Coca-Cola in its day, is now a feat, indeed virtually impossible. In the space of a few years, we have gone from a commendable requirement for explanation to a moralizing requirement for justification.

The percentages of sugar, salt, or fat content listed on many food items just for our information threaten to turn into warnings for our consumption.

A similar thing is happening with perfumes, since most products of animal origin traditionally used in their composition are no longer utilized, in the name of morality rather than industry regulations, thus unwittingly depriving the African tribes who supplied them of revenue, and consequently condemning them to abject poverty.

Even though they have never posed any problem with toxicity, other very longstanding raw materials are no longer used as a precaution, and they are sometimes replaced with new products for which we have no objective track record, but merely tests to prove their innocuousness. More insidiously, market testing is used to justify market censorship, though it cannot hope to explain a person's choice of perfume.

Is this the great fear of our time? We are all responsible for this excessive censorship that never favors creativity, but merely hinders it.

Between Paris and Gembloux, Monday 17 May 2010

*Generosity*

Pierre Gagnaire is arranging a private dinner party in Gembloux, near Liège. Delighted and intrigued in equal measure by
the promised feast, which will bring together writers, experts in
various fields and a university dean, I immediately accept and
make my way to the Gare du Nord this Monday afternoon,
to head for Liège. On the train I meet another guest. During
the journey we chat and agree that we have no idea what to
expect. But, spurred on by curiosity and affection for our host,
we have both gladly accepted the invitation. A driver is waiting
for us at the station in Liège, and he takes us to the faculty of
agronomic sciences at the university in Gembloux.

After a visit to the campus, we are shown into a greenhouse
of exotic plants where we are welcomed by Pierre and Sylvie
Gagnaire. On one side of this unusual setting (which seems to
invite us on a journey), the chef has set up his stage facing the
guests' table: a gas hob with four rings and a table by way of a
work surface. Behind it are a sink, a fridge and a few cupboards
in white wood to store plates, glasses, cutlery and utensils.

Gagnaire's guests are not merely spectators but, along with him,
actors for an evening. The play is called 'For the Joy of Taste' and
we have each been given a small notebook and a pencil to jot down
our impressions. I shall write very little this evening; I cannot live
intensely and make notes about my feelings at the same time.

The dinner begins with a tartare of langoustine and razor-shell clams with pomegranate, a subtle combination of sweet and acid flavors, followed by cod fillet nestling in a velouté sauce made with nettles, a deft interplay of masks in which the greenness of the nettles disguises the tender flesh of the fish. Next come fresh morels flavored with liquorice, the woodland tastes and the bitterness of liquorice root in perfect harmony, then courgette flowers served with white asparagus tips. We are still in the realm of tender, slightly bitter flavors. The dinner continues with a pea and baby broad bean soup with red olive-filled ravioli, flavored with castoreum, accompanied by a wine with the same feral tones and hints of raspberry.

We are a third of the way through the menu. Pierre Gagnaire is completely focused on his cooking, bringing pans up to his nose, smelling them, listening to them, putting them back down and stirring their contents with a finger to check the temperature. All his senses are alert. We talk among ourselves and with him, our conversations punctuated by applause, bravos and hurrahs. The only obvious sign of exertion: his increasingly unruly hair, which testifies to the effort he is going to, and gives some idea of the pleasures he is affording us. He has to change his apron several times during the course of the evening.

The meal began at nine o'clock, and it is now two o'clock in the morning. Our aesthetic appetites are gratified by the menu's boundless imagination; we are physically sated. The desserts are to be concise; after such generosity, sweet things are almost uncalled for. Pierre has not left the stage for five hours. Five hours of generosity. His cuisine is not a response to a need, but a loving dialogue. And that certainly is art.

On the plane, then in Cabris, Friday 28 May 2010

*Shameful smells*

The woman next to me on the flight is wearing Van Cleef &
Arpels' *First*. Her perfume is struggling to cover the smell of
cigarettes impregnating her clothes. Sitting beside her, her husband jolts with occasional bouts of hiccups, which release the
smell of undigested garlic.

My acute sense of smell means I can detect and identify all
sorts of odors that may be intended to be secret or hidden. It
is not unusual for me to discern alcohol, tobacco, sweat, breath
or strong food; they are all easy for me to pick up and are not
necessarily unpleasant.

Whereas the images we receive are exterior to us, smells actually penetrate us. This can be experienced as a breach of our
person, and psychologists believe this forms the basis for the
pleasure, displeasure or even disgust a particular smell can elicit.
In everyday life, we are more tolerant of our own smells and those
of our nearest and dearest than we are of other people's. And yet
they eat, defecate, urinate, sweat, make love and live like everyone
else. In fact, our olfactory rejections often stem from differences
in diet, which alter body odor and therefore involuntarily create
distance. When it comes to changing our own baby's nappies,
we happily delegate the task, although we may then be eager to
nuzzle every fold of the warm and duly cleaned little body. Once
the mashed baby food phase is over, the child's smell will match
that of the rest of the family whose diet he or she now shares.

I'm always struck by the immutable tradition in old American films that portrays women taking a long time to prepare in the bathroom before love-making: the man lies on the bed waiting, while his partner emerges showered, smelling of nothing but perfume. Alongside this prudish example from 1950s films, I am reminded of Albert Cohen's novel *Belle du Seigneur*, in which Ariane and Solal are determined to perpetuate the passion of their first meeting, a permanently insatiable love in which the smell of their bodies has to be mastered to express their purity.

> She said thank you, said she would think about it, that she would give her answer later, after another bath, a bath in pure water, yes, dear friend, an odorless bath, because the perfumed salts of her earlier bath smelled far too strong [. . .] Constantly washing, shaving twice a day, always being handsome, that had been his aim in life for the last three months.

Another memory comes to mind. Two years ago, in July, I drove some visitors through the Hautes Alpes region to see the fields of lavender and smell the clary sage. When we had reached the austere and beautiful site, some of the guests climbed swiftly back into the bus to get away from the human sweat smell of the sage that the wind was wafting into our nostrils. I myself was quite happy for these flowers to give me the smell of my own bestiality, my non-eternity, the smell of life.

Yes, I like smells that are not so easy to talk about, the ones it is seen as indecent or even disturbing to mention. As a composer of perfumes, I delight in them and play with them. Birch-tar, castoreum, Atlas cedar, civet, cumin, indole, jasmine, labdanum, oak moss, clary sage, skatole . . . all are extracts and molecules that mimic or hide smells from our bodies.

From Van Cleef & Arpels' *First* to *Voyage d'Hermès*, in every instance I have taken pleasure in using these elements of artifice and revelation to emphasize what is specific to each of us: our own smell.

Cabris, whenever

*Inheritance*

I 'met' Edmond Roudnitska in 1966 on the day my father gave me an enchanting booklet with a cover illustration of a bouquet of flowers against a black background. The German perfumery company Dragoco had devoted its entire review, *Dragoco Report*, to Edmond Roudnitska. The title was: 'The Young Perfume Composer and Smells.' That year Roudnistska created *Eau Sauvage* for Christian Dior. At the time I knew his son, and it was thanks to him that, a few months later, Edmond Roudnitska invited me to his house in Cabris. I don't remember that first meeting, except that he was friendly.

In the late 1970s I contacted him, buoyed by my experience as a perfumer. I hoped to overcome my shyness and prove my worth during the course of our conversation. I arranged the meeting by telephone, for four o'clock in the afternoon – the time recommended by his wife Thérèse. Our conversation absolutely had to end before a particular television game show called *Des chifres et des lettres*.[4] He liked to shut himself away and join in with the game, which he carried on watching until the end of his life. So I arrived at precisely four o'clock. He opened the door to me and immediately berated me: 'You reek of washing powder! Go and wash and come back tomorrow in clothes that have been aired.'

---

[4] 'Numbers and letters' – the equivalent of *Countdown* in Britain.

I found this greeting disconcerting, but it did nothing to dampen my determination. I showed up again the next day, in the same clothes. He gave me a friendly welcome. His office was level with the garden and we had to go downstairs to get to it. There were test blotters waiting to be smelled on a side table in the hallway. The room itself was huge with a large bay window looking out on to the garden. On his desk there were no bottles, no test blotters, nothing to disturb the neutral smell of the room, just a few sheets of paper and some pencils.

He introduced me to his dog, a chow he was very proud of, and explained that every time he shampooed the dog, he rinsed it down in a vinegary solution to get rid of all the odors. To be honest, I thought it still smelled quite strongly – but it was not my dog. I made no comment, not wanting to risk being cornered into an argument about my clothes and their reek of washing powder.

He talked about simplicity, about 'form' in the Platonic sense of the word, and about *qualia*, a philosophical concept he was the first to apply to perfume. His aim was to capture the olfactory image of each raw material in order to set up a sort of Pantone of smells, establishing what he hoped would be a definitive chart. We then spent a while trying to find the exact words to define the smell of phenyl ethyl alcohol, a synthesized compound that smells of wilted roses and sake. But the thing I remember most clearly is the performance he put on as he escorted me back to the door. He started singing opera arias, explaining that he had always dreamed of becoming a baritone.

We met several times. Then, after reading an article of his published in a specialist review, I wrote him a long letter describing him as 'dogmatic,' which, to my mind, was not a criticism, but he did take umbrage. He replied rather frostily, wondering who had rattled my cage. He indicated that I would no longer be invited to his house and that there would be no more conversations. I am very happy to say that three years later a mutual friend dispelled the misunderstanding and arranged for us to meet again. Edmond invited me to Cabris. We resumed our discussions, and he confided in me that he was having problems communicating with, and being taken seriously by, the young marketing directors of the companies for which he worked. To him perfume was an art. The only response he hoped for was approval from those who had commissioned him. How could he pay attention to the rumblings of 'market pressures'?

I inherited something from him (and inheritances that are chosen are the most generous): the notion of form, and a will to strive for simplicity, achieved by composing short formulae using a restricted collection. Where he was rigorous, I prefer moderation, which does not preclude exacting expectations. On the other hand, I managed to break away from a classic type of harmony expressed in the proportions of the raw materials, because I was convinced that the interplay of smells was more important. Like him, I think we need to talk and write about our craft, about which the general public knows so little. Perfume is at the heart of our lives.

*Heritage*

I cannot evoke the memory of Edmond Roudnitska without mentioning heritage. My father was a perfumer, but we spoke little of his work at home: it was his territory, and that was the rule; the make-up of my olfactory memory, therefore, derives in large part from unwittingly copying his habit of smelling any food or drink before tasting it. There was not one piece of fruit, one dish, salad, vinaigrette, slice of bread, glass of wine or even of water that escaped this olfactory moment of truth. My mother loathed this behavior and thought it contravened the good manners she was trying to instill in us. But when as many smells pass under our noses as images before our eyes, I like to remember the importance he gave to the role played by our noses.

In the late 1950s my mother wore *Madame Rochas*. Judging this perfume today, I would say it is a lovely, slightly quaint construction of florals and amber; but the image that has stayed with me is that it smelled 'too much' of perfume. This created a distance and elicited respect. Sometimes I dared to open the bottle secretly in the bathroom and I discovered a sweet generous smell of faded roses and old vanilla paper. It intrigued me and helped sustain the reassuring portrait I had of a woman of bourgeois elegance, who never changed her perfume. I could not imagine her wearing another, nor allow her to do so: my mother would no longer have been my mother.

Olfactory legacies are often acquired involuntarily. For example, in the summer my paternal grandmother used to offer to help pick the crop of flowers for her neighbors, who were horticulturalists. I sometimes went with her, and spent the morning playing between rows of jasmine. I was safe in that world of flower pickers. Especially as, although I was as lazy as the cicada in La Fontaine's fable, they were more generous than the ant:[5] at the end of the morning, they each laid a handful of flowers in my basket. This meant I need not lose face when I went up to the owner, who had a notebook in which he kept a daily tally of the flowers picked; the pickers were paid at the end of the month. Since then I have not found a more sensual scent than that of bare arms on which the smell of sweat is mingled with that of jasmine flowers. In fact, I was learning the smell of perfumes and the smell of women at the same time. And leaving childhood behind without realizing it.

After a three-year stint as an unskilled worker for Antoine

Chiris, I went to Givaudan as a laboratory assistant in the late 1960s. My job consisted of weighing out formulae for three perfumers, which meant I learned the different ways of writing a formula for a perfume. There were formulae involving several dozen components as well as bases (combinations of a dozen raw materials) and subformulae (formulae within the new formula, which could themselves include bases), and these sometimes took a couple of days to prepare; and there were those that

[5] In La Fontaine's fable 'The Cicada and the Ant,' the industrious ant refuses to give food to the cicada, who has been dancing all summer rather than preparing for the winter.

comprised some fifty components and just a few bases. I soon decided which I preferred: particularly as the handwriting in the complex formulae was so small and cramped, and so laborious to read, that it made the weighing-out process take even longer.

Later, when I was starting out as a student of perfumery, my father bequeathed me two files and a box, rather like a shoe box, full of formulae. He had put a great deal of care into preparing them before giving them to me. Each formula was typed out on white paper, arranged in alphabetical order and numbered. A novice in the trade, I viewed this store of knowledge as a treasure trove; the names – *Rose Tea, Opopanax, Amber Moss, Quelques Fleurs* – may well have been evocative, but the formulae meant nothing to me. Yes, I could deduce their complexity, but I could not read them, even less imagine them as smells. To a young man of the 1968 generation, these formulae belonged to the past, a past I wanted to break away from as everyone was doing at the time. I have never reread them; they live in a plastic storage box. Nowadays I have a different experience when I read old books of perfume formulae, devised from the late nineteenth century up to the present day. And it is one of my dreams that they will one day be studied and made public, to show that perfume is the result of complex intellectual activity, work involving the mind, and not some haphazard combination of smells.

Cabris, Tuesday 8 June 2010

*Afternoon visitors*
I have agreed to spend a few hours talking with three young perfumers. I am both delighted and apprehensive. My apprehension is because I always feel uncomfortable criticizing another perfumer's work. I cannot do it without projecting my own vision, when I should be helping them express their own. I do not know whether my visitors are bringing any perfumes they have created. They arrive on time, and before we sit down I give them a tour of the laboratory. I imagine they feel the same degree of curiosity as mine when I first visited Edmond Roudnitska's office; I remember analyzing every last detail of the place in order to understand the man and his perfumes. We come back into the living room, which acts as an office. They ask me a lot of questions about how I work, and my relationship with the marketing and evaluation departments. I tell them that here the marketing department is called 'the perfume collections development department,' and has no decision-making power in the choice of perfumes. As for an evaluating department assessing creations in terms of the market, there is none. Willing though I am to hear everyone's and anyone's reactions and to know other people's opinions, I alone can judge my creations. My visitors say they noticed perfumes from different companies in my fridge, and ask what I need these for. I explain that they are mainly there as historical benchmarks of quality, below which I must not and would not want to fall.

They have aesthetic dimensions that I value: sillage, longevity, presence, diffusion, vigor and clarity.

'I saw a bottle of *Diorissimo.*'

'It's one of my points of reference. No, it's more than that; it's among the creations I admire because it so accurately captures the difference between a smell and a perfume. Its starting point is the smell of lily of the valley. The end point for a composer of perfumes is to transform a unique smell into a perfume. In this instance, nature provides a smell that our senses can decipher. Thanks to our training, we know how to reproduce it. So we have our theme, our idea; now we have to add something of ourselves: our own desires and – this is the most complex part – our personality. When I create a perfume, I extend it with a story. I think everyone should try it. We reveal a part of ourselves when we compose a perfume. Whether the story is written before, during or after the creation, it's our story, and it supports the creative process, even though it only expresses a part of it.'

They do not show me any perfumes. I thank them for this, explaining how awkward I feel when I have to smell and judge another perfumer's work.

Cabris, Wednesday 9 June 2010

*Memory*

I have been told that a journalist from *Le Nouvel Observateur* is going to call me tomorrow in connection with an article about memory. And to think I don't trust my own memory even though I work with it!

When I was an apprentice, I used to organize memorization competitions. The exercise consisted in smelling a dozen test blotters, each of which had been dipped into one of the primary scents in the collection. The winner was the person who could identify the raw material the fastest. We managed to commit a hundred smells to memory in this way, then two hundred, then a thousand, and we were proud of our ability. We could recognize them, but we did not know them. Putting a name to a smell is not all it takes to appreciate its character, its limitations and possibilities. With the determination of an ignoramus who wants to learn everything, know everything, control everything and measure everything, I filled whole notebooks on each of them. I classified smells by type, by family, in alphabetical order and in order of their performance. The act of writing definitely helped to reinforce my memory. Sometimes if I lose my way when I am searching for ideas, I trawl through these notebooks, but I very rarely find an answer. In spite of that, I still fill them out conscientiously.

Because I constantly try to find new aspects to smells, they remain indistinct, their contours ill-defined. Smells are not like pieces of Lego that we can fit together to make a perfume, but insubstantial entities that I strive to render intelligible.

Cabris, Thursday 10 June 2010

*'The smell object'*

I take the call from the journalist. I answer her questions and
talk at length about the ways in which fragrant raw materials
are used. Building a memory means giving olfactory contours
to a smell or, to be more precise, managing to make the smell
no longer merely something that can be appreciated with the
senses but something that becomes an intelligible object, so
that it can be used, manipulated and given direction.

I have hundreds of primary scents at my disposal. Over time,
I have reduced my collection to fewer than two hundred smells
in order to pinpoint the 'smell object' as accurately as possible.
When I was starting out as a perfumer, smells were undefined,
and I had only a meager, restricted vocabulary to describe them.
By immersing myself in smells on a daily basis, my vocabulary
has become more precise and extensive.

Natural sources are complex. They have clearly defined, immutable contours which do not lend themselves to inventiveness,
but they have an advantage that I put to good use: their ability
to seduce, to envelop, to establish themselves clearly, and sometimes to be the basis for the perfume form I want to express.

Synthetic sources are more interesting because, except in a
few cases, their contours are not so defined and are therefore
more versatile and better suited to manipulations, abstraction
and creating illusions. For example, phenyl ethyl alcohol, a synthetic substance, can be used for every kind of floral note.

This smell provides a consistency, a roundedness and a tranquility that are more important than the smell of roses with which it is associated. I only have to think of phenyl ethyl alcohol, or of any of the raw materials I use, for the smell to take shape in my thoughts. This is how I avoid classifications or terminology getting in the way of smells. When smell and thought are interchangeable, then I am a composer of perfumes.

Cabris, Wednesday 16 June 2010

*Nasturtiums*

I would describe my feelings towards smells as friendship, and sometimes as an unpredictable infatuation that can veer into disappointment. When I smelled the extract of nasturtium leaves and flowers that I was given a few months ago, I was instantly filled with passion. I had been longing for some time for a lively, green smell with a distinctive character that would bring out the originality of a future idea. I set about using it in new accords and when putting the finishing touches to various projects. I felt that these accords and works in progress were flawed, but I put this down to other causes, not my use of the nasturtium concentrate. Passion blinds us, and that was the case here. Having left my trials out on the table for a few weeks to mature, I noticed that their flaws had become more pronounced and that they now had a vinegary smell, similar to that of pickled gherkins. I was forced to conclude that the nasturtiums were to blame. They disappeared from my trials and – with some regret but not without hope – I asked the supplier to look into the problem of their olfactory instability.

Cabris, Wednesday 23 June 2010

*Patience*

This morning two irises the blue of a winter sky bloomed. They flowered for the space of a morning and I hope they will flower again next year. I have been waiting for them to open for a few days. I am very attached to them, even though their beauty is banal. What speaks to me and awes me is all that patience, the slow, sustained effort to achieve their opening once a year.

To be honest, I know nothing about these irises, having brought them back from my travels when I was creating *Un Jardin après la Mousson* in 2007. When I was visiting the Kerala Hills, I remember stopping at a garden center. These places have nothing in common with our own, there is nothing exotic about them, no profusion, just a few local plants in pots, and in a barn, sheltered from the sun, a massive store of carefully categorized seeds for vegetables, flowers and medicinal plants. With a little patience and a few seeds sold by the gram, the Indians can create gardens. As I came out of the barn, I noticed a terrace edged with blue flowers that looked like irises, a variety I did not know. I asked a young Indian woman what they were called, and she was able to tell me. Intrigued, I asked her whether I could have one of the rhizomes; she hauled out a clump of irises and used a knife to cut away three rhizomes for me. Back at the hotel I wrapped them in toilet paper and slipped them into a plastic bag to keep them damp. When I arrived home, not knowing what sort of soil there was in Kerala, I put them in pots. Since then they have flowered every year in June.

There are two trials in the refrigerator waiting for me to smell them. They will reach full maturity in a week. I have been working on this theme for several years now, and I feel as if the birth is now near, in other words the perfume has achieved the form I so wanted. Rather than a smell, what I am looking for in it is a texture, a consistency, and I want it to be unusual and self-evident. I have called my trials *Narcisse bleu*. I do not yet know which one I will put forward.

Cabris, Wednesday 30 June 2010

*Resistance*

It is not the market that homogenizes olfactory premises, but what we offer it. Starting with this statement, I have begun a gradual process of resistance. So I fight against 'uniform' perfumery, the sort that trumpets its pleasantness, boasts about performance and strives to make its mark because, once normalized, it cannot go back to its roots or be reinvented.

No demonstrations or outspoken tirades; I hope to establish a serene presence for perfume. As I see it, perfume whispers to our noses, speaks to us intimately, makes connections with our thoughts. In order to express this, I bend the market rules by breaking away from the women's versus men's dogma. I do not like the terms 'unisex' or 'mixed'; usage does not define a genre. Which is why I make perfumes for sharing, novel-perfumes, novella-perfumes and poem-perfumes.

Cabris, Thursday 1 July 2010

*Cost*

In response to market demand, I tend to formulate a perfume with materials that come at a high price, and using an important variable: concentration. I prefer quality over quantity, because I do not believe that excessive concentration in a perfume or longevity on the skin are necessarily proof of quality. I have met many women who cannot smell their own perfume, although my nose felt they had applied excessive amounts. I am all in favor of the notion of abundance, plenty and richness being a perfume's aesthetic expression, but when its olfactory performance – its diffusion and staying power – is the 'plus point,' then its performance in other terms is inevitably poor.

Cabris, Friday 2 July 2010

*Launch*

For the launch of *Iris Ukiyoé*, we have invited a few journalists to the Maeght Foundation in Saint-Paul-de-Vence. I am
delighted with this opportunity to introduce a perfume in such
a setting. It gives me a chance to talk about my interest in Japanese culture and its influence on Western culture to this day.
I mention the concepts of fullness and emptiness. Fullness,
which is so dear to the West where the subject of a painting
fills the entire canvas, leaving little room for individual imagination, where the eye is led from left to right and the idea of
the work, once grasped, is fixed for all eternity. Emptiness,
which is valued in Japanese art, where the subject floats and
dissolves into and on the surface of the paper, leaving gaps
and spaces for individual projection, in which artists celebrate
nature, life, the seasons and other forms of eternity.

I talk about the different mindsets of painting with oils, or
water-based inks; about oil in the West, about working with a
colored substance, its richness, the feel of it, its excess and density; and about water for Japan, about impregnating the paper,
black ink in all its nuances, about simplicity, clean lines and telling gestures.

I am not trying to pit the two cultures against each other,
merely to explain my stylistic choices (which echo Japanese art)
and my desire to 'wrong-foot' the nose.

Cabris, Wednesday 7 July 2010

Féminin H, *continued*

While I am tidying up the things on my desk this morning, I smell a forgotten test blotter for *Féminin H*. I notice an effect I previously missed, one I find bewitching and sensual, and which entices me to embark on a new path. I put to one side the work based on pears and keep the words 'appetizing' and 'crisp' as guiding principles, expressing them this time with an accord I am fond of with slightly acid blackberry–grape–red-currant notes. I associate this with the commonplace elegance of patchouli and other molecules that work together well. The first trial has a rather muddled form with the high percentage of patchouli playing out alone and producing the effect of a camphorated refrigerant as it begins to evaporate, but then melting away pleasantly after a few minutes. The overall impression is seductive. The proportions will stay as they are. I simply correct the juxtaposition of smells by adding some woody notes. This trial is an open invitation to continue along the same route.

Cabris, Thursday 8 July 2010

*Sixth sense*

To conclude his article, a Dutch journalist asks me whether I have a sixth sense. 'Perhaps a sense of time,' I reply. I should have said, 'a feeling for time.'

In the 1990s, I held the position of head perfumer and had a team working for me. I remember a very heated exchange with one perfumer after I had smelled one of his creations. I criticized his style, which emulated the style of the 1970s. He replied that the 70s were the golden age of perfumery and this was how he liked to work. It was his point of view. I might have understood and even accepted it if he'd been a free agent. But I stated emphatically that I could not accept his reply because our clients, who had entrusted us with this commission, were looking for perfumes with a contemporary spirit.

Ever since that exchange, I find myself smelling my work with a lurking fear that my compositions have a fragrance only for the present. I am wary of nostalgia; it confers on perfumes a complacent seductiveness. I cannot predict the future, and those who try often get it wrong. In fact, I am not aiming to be sidelined, but outside fashions, trends and time, and yet of the present.

Cabris, Wednesday 21 July 2010

*Style*

Having worked hard to define a style for my compositions, a way of writing perfume, I know that there is a danger of being overly faithful to myself. Repetition leads to caricature, stagnation and even exhaustion. By restricting myself to one premise, I run the risk of no longer being heard or watched with anticipation. Conversely, if I listen too much and am too influenced by trends, I rapidly condemn myself to being part of the 'contemporary scene' and losing my individuality. More than once I have allowed myself to overcomplicate things and to be very slapdash with my formulae, only to throw my work away, forget about it and start all over again in order to find my way. With the balance of a tightrope walker, I have to hear without necessarily listening. I may be acutely aware of what I am doing, but I also value doubt, and I nurture it: I know no better aid to the creative process.

Cabris, Thursday 22 July 2010

*Tinkering*

The industry now has analytical tools that I find wonderful: chromatographs, spectrographs, computers. I have played with them for hours, trying to find 'the' molecule that gave a smell its meaning. An innocent approach when we know that the scent of a rose comprises hundreds of different molecules and that not one of them smells like a rose. So I have not found 'the' rose molecule, but I have discovered that the smells of flowers have a biologically dictated cycle, and that their composition can vary significantly without them losing their identity – and this has altered the way I envisaged the process of composing perfumes. Thanks to these analytical instruments, I have also learned how perfumes could be constructed. Since I stopped using them, I have abandoned analysis, favoring a more sensitive approach, tinkering with ingredients and quantities.

Perfume is not a product of science, even if it is backed up by it. There is an element of tinkering in the way a perfume is constructed; illusions and olfactory decoys play their part. I make slow progress, tentatively feeling my way with successive trials. My collection may be limited, but in my cupboards I have boxes and boxes of raw materials that I like but never use, although they do have a role: they are in the back of my mind as the 'it might be useful.' I keep them because the judgment I have passed on them is not final. They could one day end up in a formula and become part of the collection, although that rarely happens.

In general, industrialization has reduced the tinkering. Right up until the 1970s, perfumers were still using powdered dried blood, tobacco cuttings and sheep droppings macerated in a soup of chemicals to reproduce the smell of musk, and moth-balls were incorporated into perfumes to recreate the smell of fur; all of which proves that perfumers certainly have a talent for tinkering. I do not regret the passing of these ingredients; I simply embrace this mentality, which is a form of creativity.

Spéracèdes, Friday 23 July 2010

*Holidays*

I am closing up my workshop for three weeks. As I shut the
door behind me, I remember the judicious choice I made six
years ago to work far away from the decision-making center.
This choice may have been partly due to my own origins, but it
also highlighted the fact that I wanted to create without being
inconvenienced by daily interruptions, and I wanted to avoid
the frenzy or anxiety generated by weekly indicators: sales fig-
ures, market share and standing within the industry. Not that
I have no interest in them – I am kept regularly informed, and
I worry about them, delight in them, and actively participate
in discussions about company strategy. All the same, I believe
that the best way to develop creativity is to work alone and
without evaluation, which does not mean without any dialogue. The majority of ideas are the fruit of assiduous, day-
to-day work, sometimes the result of meeting people, country
walks, idle strolls, things I have read, moments when my mind
is free to roam. My moleskin notebook, in which I jot down
ideas, words and the beginnings of formulae, is always close
at hand.

But being alone also means knowing how to manage solitude
and the risk of losing momentum that can come with it. I always
have several projects, several formulae, on the go. Having a work
routine, keeping to a timetable and setting goals for myself are

all devices I use to counter that tendency to withdraw. I experience solitude as a freedom I have chosen. It is balanced out by
my regular trips to Paris.

Spéracèdes, Wednesday 28 July 2010

*The dream perfume*

I am continuing this diary during the holidays in the light-hearted spirit of a summer magazine. I have never answered the question 'What would be your dream perfume?' for lack of time to develop a clear answer. I will have a try today.

The dream perfume is one that can be smelled and experienced in the moment, for the time of one inhalation, but not one to be worn. It is not an ornament, or an item of clothing, nor is it a protection. It is pure emotion. This concept might be confusing because imagining a perfume in this way takes us outside its usual codes. I dream up perfume as a poetic offering, a 'sudden ravishing delight of unpredictability' in the words of haiku-writers, who reveal the unknown at the very heart of the familiar. I came close to this dream in Japan, when I took part in a Kodo ceremony. These complex ceremonies involving perfume and incense can take different forms. During this one, the master of ceremonies burned ten different fragrances one after another. For each fragrance, the participants were invited to compose a poem – in English for the *gaijins* (foreigners) – and to hand their writings to the master of ceremonies. All the poems were read by him, and those attending were asked to choose the poem that best evoked the perfume. The winner was whoever was selected the most often. The ceremony followed a slow, precise and coded ritual. Despite the discomfort of sitting cross-legged on a tatami for more than two hours, I found that this meshing of poetry and smells generated in me feelings of completeness and harmony – an experience shared by most of the participants.

The dream can take another form. I sometimes think I should go back to some of my perfumes and rewrite them. I do not mean starting with the same theme and creating a new perfume, which is something I have already done on the theme of tea, for example. But rather to have a similar approach to making a new translation of a book, staying as close as possible to the original perfume, but writing it with other words – smells – that might translate the idea I now have of the perfume.

The way in which we read and perceive a book is not exactly the same today as it was yesterday, and the same can be said of perfume. Chanel's rewriting of *No. 5* with *Eau Première* was an interesting way of interpreting this idea. If I pursue a similar dream, though, I am not sure I will find any takers.

Spéracèdes, Monday 2 August 2010

*Accords*
*(Combinations of several sounds heard together and creating a harmony.)*
In the beginning was the image of a piano with its eighty-eight keys. If I press all the keys at the same time, it makes an unpleasant noise. Mixing eighty-eight unselected components is highly likely to produce exactly the same sort of olfactory 'noise.' Now, if I play just three keys at random on the piano, how many different possibilities are there on an eighty-eight-key keyboard? One hundred and nine thousand seven hundred and thirty-six, according to mathematical calculation. If I transfer that calculation to the number of possible accords from dipping three test blotters at random in a collection of primary scents, even a modest one, the possibilities are considerable.

I realize this is a simplistic image and that, if I chose the components, many accords could be avoided because I would anticipate those that would not be worth making. Even so, I think the metaphor is an amusing way of illustrating the need to formulate things with simplicity.

I do not know how many components there need to be before a formula is called 'complex.' I only know that this sort of formula is very likely to reuse known accords, which appeals to commercial perfumers.

I am, therefore, against complicated formulae, in which repetitions and accumulations give a muddled and unintelligible –

though seductive – reading. I prefer simplicity; it alone allows for new readings of the same premise, but I consent to complexity when it affords subtlety. The perfume *Bois Farine* that I created for L'Artisan Parfumeur is a simple formula, comprising about ten components, yet it is complex because it uses a base that contains thiazoles and pyrazines, which are difficult and, in some cases, unstable chemical compounds, and can only be used in very diluted forms.

Spéracèdes, Friday 6 August 2010

*Bees*

'What color stripe do you start with to draw a bee?' When my grandson asked me this question I was at first surprised, then dazzled. Surprised because I had never thought to ask this myself, and dazzled because it was about a minor detail that was not, in fact, minor at all as it pertained to millions of bees. I told him I did not know and that he could color his picture however he liked. I regret that I could not give him an answer. His question denoted a concern to find the truth, an attentive eye and a curious mind. We could have looked for images of bees together on the internet and found an answer – there was bound to be one. Later in the day I opened my moleskin notebook and wrote down the question; it is an example of the child's view that we should all try to nurture in our own thought processes.

Cabris, Tuesday 17 August 2010

*Back to work*

The first thunderstorm breaks sometime around the 15<sup>th</sup> of August every year. I like listening to the thunder; it's one of the most beautiful drum rolls. The grey of the clouds gives some green back to the trees. The rain sets free all the smells that the sun condemned. The months of intense heat are over. There is something reassuring about this renewal.

This morning the sky is spreading out its blue above the workshop. I open the door after three weeks away. The smell hits me. Despite all our precautions, the place is fragrant. I had forgotten that I am cloaked in this smell all year long. I think about visitors encountering it for the first time. It is a presence, a distinctive feature. I know that I need it.

Cabris, Wednesday 18 August 2010

Féminin H, *still*

It is a pleasure to get back to the latest work on *Féminin H*; the trials are promising. The inclusion of sandalwood has smoothed the coarse camphor effect of the patchouli. The overall form is full, dense and elegant; but it is not airy enough. I embark on some trials with different types of patchouli that I had put to one side 'just in case.' An ester of patchouli gives good results because it has the earthy notes of the traditional essential oil. I carry on with my trials, changing the quality of the musk I originally used, to improve its longevity. At this stage, my task is that of a craftsman perfecting a completed piece. It is systematic work during which I experiment with the different qualities of some of the raw materials used in the formula, paying closer attention to the technical aspects – diffusion, persistence and presence. Later I will put more work into achieving crispness and gorgeousness, and the mischievous smile I want this perfume to have.

Cabris, Friday 20 August 2010

*Changing direction*

Language lives freely and quite independently of us, and, over time, the words that make it up alter their meaning. (Until recently the word *'escagasser'* – which is originally an Occitan word and has a ring to it that I love – meant only to stun or knock senseless; now it can also mean to bore (to death).) The same is true of smells, which can change their meaning over time, without actually losing any of their former significance.

Unlike with language, where no individual can single-handedly change the meaning of a word, when a perfumer puts forward a new interpretation of a smell, he can change its significance. For example, the smell of ionone beta – a molecule discovered in 1893 – was synonymous with the smell of violets right up to the end of the twentieth century. In order to create the accord with tea in *Eau parfumée au thé vert* for Bulgari, I used this synthetic compound in a different way and combined ionone beta with hedione. The perfume became a market archetype, and the smell changed: Ionone no longer smells just of violets, but also of tea.

In the Hermès perfume *Poivre Samarcande*, traces of absolute of violet leaves combined with a high dosage of iso E reveal the peppery aspect of this molecule, hitherto unrecognized. Phenyl ethyl alcohol, used since it was first discovered to evoke the smell of roses, is now used to evoke the smell of sake or cooked rice.

I know that words, and even more so smells, do not have the same significance for each of us; all the same, smells are elements that perfumers can transform, bring to life and change. It is because they change meaning that they are alive, and that perfumes are alive.

Cabris, Tuesday 24 August 2010

*Narcisse bleu*

A work meeting about current projects. We have a lengthy discussion about the composition of *Narcisse bleu*, an improvisation that I am putting forward for the Cologne collection. I explain that, although the smell is important, what I am particularly hoping to express in this perfume is the tactile aspect.

A perfume never speaks to one sense alone, but offers itself to all the senses. In saying that, I do not mean its name, the packaging or the bottle, but the perfume's smell. I am reminded of Paul Cézanne who said that, from its colors, he could tell whether an object was velvety, hard or soft and even what it smelled like. I found my subject in the smell of narcissi. Not the flower, which hovers between the fragrance of roses, white flowers and horse droppings, but an extract obtained from the flowers as well as the stalks, which – for me – has a green, abrasive, rounded, powdery smell. With a juxtaposition of green, abrasive, powdery, woody and floral notes, I have interpreted this olfactory perception by playing on contrasts between the abrasive, powdery and woody notes, and the green and floral ones. Narcissus may be the main premise of this cologne, but I will not actually be using an extract of it, because I am trying to achieve a density and a thickness that only synthesized compounds can give me, because their characteristics can melt together without detracting from the way the subject is interpreted.

Cabris, Thursday 26 August 2010

*Mediterranean*

I was born in Grasse, and yet I do not feel Grassois by nature, nor Provençal, for that matter. My parents and I left Grasse too early for me to feel I belong in the town, although I am fond of it. My attachment to the place is due to my paternal grandparents, who were of Italian descent and who set up home there; but also to the people who helped, taught, instructed and supported me during my apprenticeship there, people who were mostly not Grassois. As for the image of people from Provence as boastful, chauvinistic, noisy and generous – characteristics that gave Pagnol's films much of their charm – I do not recognize myself in it. I prefer Jean Giono's world. Pagnol the Parisian tended towards regionalism, Giono the Manosquin had his eye on the universal.[6]

I try to avoid the sun, and favor shady woodland. I find the languor of beaches boring, but am drawn to creeks and reefs. I love the sea and its horizon, where my gaze gets lost as the blue of the sky and that of the sea merge. I appreciate the beautiful bodies, the drape of light clothing, the discreet elegance and restraint. I have never been able to truss myself up in suits; their restrictiveness denotes a rigidness of mind and disenchantment with life. I believe in happiness, in man, in a lay spirituality; I do

[6] A Manosquin is a native of Manosque, a small town in the Alpes de Haute Provence region.

not trust religions. I would rather have eye contact for a long time than chatter for a long time. And, although I like to seduce, I have a sense of propriety with words. As I write this, I am reminded in particular of Camus, who wrote in *L'exil d'Hélène*:

> 'Greek thought always took refuge in the idea of limits. It pushed nothing to its full extent, not the sacred, nor reason, because it denied nothing, not the sacred, nor reason. It took everything into account, balancing shadow with light.'

I have never sought to impose anything. My research is driven by a constant desire to find a balance between what can be felt with the senses and what is intelligible to the mind. I am Mediterranean.

Cabris, Wednesday 1 September 2010

*Subject*

A perfume does not necessarily need a subject, a concept; if it is beautiful it exists in itself. *Un Jardin en Méditerranée* was created with a subject as its starting point: the smell of fig leaves, which represent the Mediterranean for me. *Terre d'Hermès* evolved differently. At the start, the only pointer I had from my chair- woman was the word *'terre'* (earth). This name had been registered as a trademark for a perfume several years previously. Clearly, it was not a question of reproducing the smell of earth. I began with a perfume structure that I had kept in reserve, one created without a subject in mind, and one I believed in. As the composition included a high percentage of woody notes, I came up with the image of a wooden post driven into the ground against the background of an Irish landscape. The post symbolized man's presence, man on earth.

As I work for a company, I do not create only for myself; I make it my duty to explain what I am doing and to establish a sincere dialogue, which airs my doubts and convictions, and can also be reassuring. *Terre d'Hermès* took eight months of work. Along the way, I sustained the creative process with dialogues and olfactory images, and later these were used in the launch brochure and to train sales staff. The subject assumed its definitive form with the final trial. It is not the hundreds of trials that prove the value of this work, even though they were necessary, but the gradual process.

I have managed to create some perfumes in less than a week, others in several months; some have been works in progress for several years, and I keep them to one side because they do not match the idea I have in mind. What I do know is that I give a great deal when I feel free.

Cabris, Friday 3 September 2010

*Tools (objects used in everyday life)*
Nowadays, most perfumes are made of ambroxan, phenyl ethyl alcohol, citronellol, coumarin, hedione, heliotropine, hydroxy-citronellal, iso E, ionone, lilial, methyl ionone, synthesized musk, patchouli, synthesized sandalwood, salicylate and vanillin. What dictates this choice of products is their unchanging characteristics, their linearity. They are fragrant substances manufactured in vast quantities and used in all perfumes: they are tools.

A century ago, these odorous compounds were new to perfumers' noses. It took intuition and repeated trials to find their uses. Then, once every combination had been tried out, perfume composers sought to use these olfactory substances in different ways. They are currently utilized in percentages that our predecessors would never have dared use. What they offer – their smells – has become common currency that the perfumer dresses up in all sorts of different ways. To satisfy the need for swift economic return, when marketing departments noticed how much time was wasted in this 'dressing up' process, they suggested that researchers should try to find molecules with similar smells. Which is what happened with the fifty or so synthetic musks available.

It takes about a decade for a new smell – whether naturally derived or synthetic – to become an 'olfactory convention,' and longer still for it to become common currency, a tool. Time has its uses, and so do tools, but only if they are properly used.

Cabris, Wednesday 22 September 2010

*Suggestions*

I remember that when the painter Émile Bernard described how Paul Cézanne approached watercolors, he came up with this idea: 'His method was unique, quite outside the usual technique and excessively complicated. He started with painting shadows and with an area of color that he covered with a second, larger one, then a third, until all these colors screening each other modeled the object by coloring it.' If you look closely at Cézanne's watercolors you can see that the areas of color do not completely cover each other, but are mostly juxtaposed. Their interplay creates a remarkable harmony.

I proceed in a similar fashion when 'modeling' a perfume, by freeing myself from the mind-set of proportions that I could have chosen – the wiser from previous experience – and by thinking only about the raw materials. It is the raw materials that shape a perfume; when they are juxtaposed, they set up resonances. When I try to establish harmony, the proportions establish themselves.

Cabris, Thursday 30 September 2010

*The moleskin notebook*

My tools are test blotters, a pencil, a block of paper and, for a number of years now, a notebook. It was as I approached forty that I started making notes on accords, ideas for perfumes, writing down thoughts, copying out quotations, at first on loose sheets of paper that piled up until I arranged them alphabetically in files of various sizes. Then there was the moleskin notebook. I like the size and shape of it because I can slip it into my pocket, like a wallet. I appreciate the elastic strap that keeps it closed, and means it can hold notes jotted quickly on to loose pages.

Because ideas and thoughts spring up freely and I do not trust my memory, I write things down. In the early days I wrote in pencil, an HB pencil, scrawling so quickly and clumsily that I had terrible trouble reading myself afterwards. I sometimes even wrote my notes out again, going to some effort, believing they were important; but they only have whatever value I give them, and that can vary. Although it made my reading less easy, I liked the idea of using pencil. There is no simpler writing implement, and I stuck to it for a few years; then, as I had more and more trouble reading what I had written, I bought an expensive fountain pen to encourage myself to write legibly. Since then, I have been decipherable. Sketches and watercolors have been added to the notebook – but only rarely. This second memory bank actually frees my mind, and allows me to concentrate on working with raw materials.

Paris, Wednesday 6 October 2010

*A composer of perfumes*

I have sought freedom in composing perfumes, and I have
been a slave to smells. I cannot stop myself smelling and
thinking about smells, for fear of losing the ability to compose.
As with all artistic work, I need to work physically with the
material and to have an understanding of it. That is the price
I pay for being a composer of perfumes, and that sometimes
worries me.

Cabris, Wednesday 13 October 2010

*Smell*

When smell is no longer linked to memory, when it no longer evokes flowers or fruits, when it is stripped of all feeling and affect, then it becomes material for a perfume.

When I can no longer describe it, when it has consistency, depth, breadth and density, when it becomes tactile, when the only representation I have of it is physical, then I can bring it to life and create.

A SUMMARY OF SMELLS

*In this summary I have reduced smells to the level of signs. This is how smells, such as amber, cherry or jasmine, are achieved using a minimum of juxtaposed materials.*

*Taken separately, the materials smell nothing like the subject headings I give.*

*This summary is essentially a game in which you subject your nose to a minimum of two test blotters sparingly impregnated with fragrance, wafting them like a barely opened fan. Sometimes, due to its intensity, one of the blotters may have to be held further away. This is not about finding proportions, but producing an interconnection, an attraction.*

*With each 'hand', I recommend smelling the blotters separately before putting them together, and I would not make more than seven smells in order to keep the nose alert. Occasionally, a combination of blotters really doesn't work for some people; you will have to experiment with how you arrange them, bringing some blotters closer or holding them further away.*

*(All materials should previously have been prepared as a 5% solution in 90° Celsius ethyl alcohol.)*

### AMBER

*Amber used in perfumery is an olfactory convention which bears no relation to the fossilized resin, yellow amber, or to ambergris, an intestinal secretion produced by sperm whales. It was the first abstract smell in perfumery and appeared at the end of the nineteenth century with the invention of vanillin. This simple juxtaposition went on to generate an extraordinary number of perfumes.*

     vanillin
     labdanum (absolute)

APPLES

*A colorful basket of apples.*

### GREEN APPLES
fructone
benzyl acetate
cis-3 hexenol

### YELLOW APPLES
fructone
hexyl acetate
benzyl acetate

### RED APPLES
fructone
allyl caproate
hexyl acetate

## CACHOU

*Although the name* cachou *may not mean much to English readers, there are similar bitter, minty lozenges in many countries, and they are a part of my childhood. My maternal grandmother carried* cachous *in her black handbag, and offered me some every time I saw her. I tasted them, and then swiftly went off to hide and spit them out. As a child, I did not like bitter tastes.*

     anethol
     ionone
     methyl cyclopentenolone
     menthol

## CANDYFLOSS

*Whether it is white, pink or green, candyfloss is more a smell associated with carnivals and children's amusements than a taste – because then it is merely sugar.*

vanillin
ethyl maltol

## CARAMEL

*Absolute of tonka bean and bezoin resinoid both evoke caramel. The olfactory illusion is perfected by associating vanillin and methyl cyclopentenolone.*

      tonka bean (absolute)
      vanillin
      methyl cyclopentenolone

CHERRY

*I like cherries picked straight from the tree, perhaps because they are a symbol of spring, but mainly because they are crisp, acidic and sugary. The taste we remember is mostly the flavor in, say, yogurts, and this condemns us to the same bland olfactory reference.*

    beta ionone
    heliotropine
    benzaldehyde

## CHOCOLATE

*The aroma of cocoa beans alone is made up of hundreds of molecules, but, by roasting the beans, man has given this distinctive flavor a very human complexity because he has tripled the number of odorous components. This juxtaposition of smells demonstrates that perfumers are above all illusionists.*

> isobutyl phenyl acetate
> vanillin

*To 'make' plain chocolate, I recommend adding patchouli; for a ganache, a trace of civet; for 'orangette',[7] orange zest; for an After Eight, spearmint; and for the smell of cocoa powder, concrete of iris.*

[7] A confection of chocolate-coated bitter orange.

FIG

*Stemone gives an impression of mint leaves or fig leaves, it all depends on what I want to make it say.*

stemone

gamma-octalactone

*For the smell of ripe figs, I recommend adding ethyl maltol, but for dried figs the answer lies in concrete of iris.*

## GARDENIA

*The gardenia perfume I like best is Chanel's, because it does not smell of the flower but of happiness. The fragrance of gardenias is a drama played out somewhere between jasmine and tuberose.*

aldehyde C-18 prunolide
styrallyl acetate
methyl anthranilate

## GRAPEFRUIT

*If there is one disappointment for perfumers, it must be grapefruit because, although it has its own essence, this essence smells of oranges. Fortunately, our arsenal includes sufficient artifice to satisfy the enthusiast.*

        sweet orange (essence)
        rhubofix

## HYACINTH

' . . . *The smell persists, always the same, always so precise and so de-manding, insisting that I carry on seeing images of vats of wine super-imposed over the real image of my books until the moment when I finally grasp that it is simply (but what an admirable entanglement of riches in that simplicity!), it is simply the smell of three hyacinths in flower.'* Jean *Giono in* Arcadia! Arcadia!

> phenyl ethyl alcohol
> benzyl acetate
> galbanum

*Adding indole brings the hyacinth more fully into bloom, while cis-3 hex-enol evokes hyacinths in bud.*

## JASMINE

*As a child I liked to go out at dawn and – using my thumb, index finger and middle finger – pick porcelain-white jasmine flowers, intoxicated by their light, tender, green fragrance. Towards noon, the last chalky-white petals exhaled a warm scent of orange blossom. By evening, the forgotten, yellowing flowers gave off a penetrating, animal smell of big cats.*

    benzyl acetate
    hedione
    clove bud oil
    indole
    methyl anthranilate

## LILY

*Lilies 'announce'! In the fifteenth century many paintings by Italian masters depicted the angel Gabriel handing lilies to Mary as he announces that she is to be a mother. The choice of lilies is never made innocently. Their shape and color are symbolic, but their smell also contributes to their symbolism.*

> benzyl salicylate
> phenyl ethyl alcohol
> methyl anthranilate

*Depending on botanical varieties, you can add linalool, indole or geraniol.*

### LIME BLOSSOM

*I have never succeeded in using this tree's blossom to my advantage. All I can do is fall asleep in its dark shade.*

> lilial
> undecavertol

## MANGO

*I bring it to my nose. The smell seduces me. A profusion of fragrant images, resin, orange peel, grapefruit, carrot, sweet myrrh, juniper; a smell that is fresh yet sweet, energetic yet tender. I can't resist it any longer. I let it caress my senses, overwhelming me with smells.*

> ionone
> aldehyde C-14
> blackcurrant buds (absolute)

OLIVE

*This smell describes the Mediterranean single-handedly. From black olives to olive paste, via olive oil, my nose and palate find endless connections: smells of truffles, castoreum, human smells, smells I am drawn to.*

castoreum
benzyl salicylate

*To which you can add styrax resinoid and thyme if you want to produce the taste of olive paste.*

## PEAR

*This Friday several stalls are selling winter pears, small crimson-colored pears whose fragrance reigns over the market . . .*

> fructone
> hexyl acetate
> rose (essence)

## PINEAPPLE

*This exotic fruit needs few elements to express itself. A simple molecule called allyl hexanoate smells of pineapple, but also evokes some kinds of apple; there are sometimes tenuous differences between two smells. To get the pineapple smell just right it is important to add ethyl maltol.*

allyl hexanoate
ethyl maltol

## PISTACHIO

*I think you have to be a Turk truly to know the taste of pistachios. On every street corner in Istanbul, traders go to ingenious lengths to build pink hills of pistachios on their stalls, and they make little paper cornets to sell fifty kurus' worth of them.*

> benzoic aldehyde
> phenylacetic aldehyde
> vanillin

## RASPBERRY

*Unlike cherries, which have more taste than smell, raspberries are all about smell.*

> fructone
> beta ionone
> frambinone

*Adding cis-3 hexenol gives a sour, green quality, while geraniol will give a taste of lipstick.*

### STRAWBERRY

*As an apprentice perfumer, I learned that the smell of strawberries could be made with C-16 aldehyde, which is known as 'strawberry' — both terms are misnomers because chemically it is in fact acetone, and it smells mainly of apples. I would suggest another combination:*

> fructone
> ethyl maltol

*And for wild strawberries:*

> fructone
> ethyl maltol
> methyl anthranilate

## SUGARED ALMONDS

*I asked a girl on work experience with me to create the smell of sugared almonds in a few words. She bought a hundred grams of the best sugared almonds from a confectioner, and this is what she wrote:*

vanillin
benzoin (resinoid)
benzaldehyde

## ACKNOWLEDGEMENTS

I would like to take this opportunity to thank the people who encouraged me to write, and those who read this diary at different stages in its development – some of them even on several occasions – and who demonstrated their friendship with their suggestions and comments. My thanks for this generosity go to: Susannah, Annelise Roux, Julie Gazier, François Simon, Marie-Dominique Lelièvre, Olivier Monteil, Catherine Fulconis, Quentin Bertoux and Stéphane Wargnier.